Fulfillment of the Holy Day and New Moon Sacrifices

Third Edition

The amazing insight into the fulfillment of the annual Holy Days and monthly New Moon sacrifices by Jesus Christ and the Churches of God.

Pieter C Voges

Contents

Disclaimer

© 2023, Author P. Voges

This eBook is designed to provide information and motivation to our readers. It may contain links to other websites or content belonging to or originating from third parties or links to websites and features. Such external links are not investigated, monitored, or checked for accuracy, adequacy, validity, reliability, availability or completeness.

All information in this eBooks is provided in good faith, however we make no representation or warranty of any kind, express or implied, regarding the accuracy, adequacy, validity, reliability, availability, or completeness of any information.

Photos are provided to assist in comprehension, but are not from actual events. They are from royalty free stock photos.

Introduction to Part 1

The Lamb of God came to fulfill many aspects of the Law so that we can understand the road to salvation and eternal life, and convert to true Christianity in all its glory and fulfillment. As our sacrificial Lamb, Christ secured salvation for all people that would follow in His footsteps. We can reach out to eternal life through the preordained path to salvation. He said so in His discussions with the apostles.

> "17 ¶ Think not that I am come to destroy the law, or the prophets: I am not come to destroy, but to fulfill."
> (Matthew 5:17, AV)

Few understand to what extend Jesus Christ fulfilled the Law, to secure salvation for us mortals. Jesus came as the sacrificial Lamb. This is what John the Baptist understood.

> "29 ¶ The next day John seeth Jesus coming unto him, and saith, Behold the Lamb of God, which taketh away the sin of the world."
> (John 1:29, AV)

To be the Lamb of God, Jesus had to fulfill the lamb sacrifices of the Holy Days and New Moons. How is that achieved? As we shall see shortly, in a most dramatic way! God does things through His predetermined ways and purposes. It was planned and executed precisely according to His plan! The apostle Paul understood this, and taught these incredible truths, from the books of Moses, from the Law, and the Prophets:

> "23 ¶ And when they had appointed him a day, there came many to him into his lodging; to whom he expounded and testified the kingdom of God, persuading them concerning Jesus, both out of the law of Moses, and out of the prophets, from morning till evening."
> (Acts 28:23, AV)

The New Moons teach us the story of how we need to respond to those sacrifices to reach up to Him and attain salvation. The Church then also sacrifices time and effort. This is also required for our salvation.

We continue in this book to reveal the insights that the first-century disciples were privileged to understand.

Chapter 1

Understanding the Festivals

In Leviticus 23, we are given a summary of the festivals. It starts with the Passover and ends with the Feast of Tabernacles. At this point, it will be useful to just read through these events to get it all in mind, before we provide some background information that is not in the average Bible.

Passover

"¶ These are the feasts of the LORD, even holy convocations, which ye shall proclaim in their seasons.
5 In the fourteenth day of the first month at even is the LORD'S passover."
(Leviticus 23:4-5, AV)

The religious year starts with the Passover. In the yearly cycle, this is the beginning of the festival season.

"6 And on the fifteenth day of the same month is the feast of unleavened bread unto the LORD: seven days ye must eat unleavened bread.

7 In the first day ye shall have an holy
convocation: ye shall do no servile work
therein.
8 But ye shall offer an offering made by
fire unto the LORD seven days: in the
seventh day is an holy convocation: ye
shall do no servile work therein."
(Leviticus 23:6-8, AV)

Right after the Passover, the seven days of the Feast
of Unleavened bread begin. Within this week, a significant
festival happens. It always happens on the day after the
weekly Sabbath that falls within the seven days of
Unleavened Bread.

"9 And the LORD spake unto Moses,
saying,
10 Speak unto the children of Israel, and
say unto them, When ye be come into the
land which I give unto you, and shall reap
the harvest thereof, then ye shall bring a
sheaf of the firstfruits of your harvest unto
the priest:
11 And he shall wave the sheaf before the
LORD, to be accepted for you: on the
morrow after the [weekly] sabbath the
priest shall wave it.
12 And ye shall offer that day when ye
wave the sheaf an he lamb without
blemish of the first year for a burnt
offering unto the LORD.
13 And the meat offering thereof shall be
two tenth deals of fine flour mingled with

oil, an offering made by fire unto the
LORD for a sweet savour: and the drink
offering thereof shall be of wine, the fourth
part of an hin.
14 And ye shall eat neither bread, nor
parched corn, nor green ears, until the
selfsame day that ye have brought an
offering unto your God: it shall be a
statute for ever throughout your
generations in all your dwellings."
(Leviticus 23:9-14, AV)

This Wave Sheaf Offering was fulfilled by Christ,
as we shall see later. From this festival, the days are
counted to Pentecost.

"15 ¶ And ye shall count unto you from
the morrow after the Sabbath, from the
day that ye brought the sheaf of the wave
offering; seven sabbaths shall be complete:
16 Even unto the morrow after the
seventh Sabbath shall ye number fifty
days; and ye shall offer a new meat
offering unto the LORD.
17 Ye shall bring out of your habitations
two wave loaves of two tenth deals: they
shall be of fine flour; they shall be baken
with leaven; they are the firstfruits unto
the LORD.
18 And ye shall offer with the bread seven
lambs without blemish of the first year,
and one young bullock, and two rams:
they shall be for a burnt offering unto the

LORD, with their meat offering, and their drink offerings, even an offering made by fire, of sweet savour unto the LORD.
19 Then ye shall sacrifice one kid of the goats for a sin offering, and two lambs of the first year for a sacrifice of peace offerings.
20 And the priest shall wave them with the bread of the firstfruits for a wave offering before the LORD, with the two lambs: they shall be holy to the LORD for the priest.
21 And ye shall proclaim on the selfsame day, that it may be an holy convocation unto you: ye shall do no servile work therein: it shall be a statute for ever in all your dwellings throughout your generations.
22 And when ye reap the harvest of your land, thou shalt not make clean riddance of the corners of thy field when thou reapest, neither shalt thou gather any gleaning of thy harvest: thou shalt leave them unto the poor, and to the stranger: I am the LORD your God."
(Leviticus 23:15-22, AV)

This concludes the first half of the festivals, normally known as the spring festivals. After this follows the second half, the fall festivals.

"23 ¶ And the LORD spake unto Moses, saying,

24 Speak unto the children of Israel,
saying, In the seventh month, in the first
day of the month, shall ye have a sabbath,
a memorial of blowing of trumpets, an
holy convocation.
25 Ye shall do no servile work therein: but
ye shall offer an offering made by fire unto
the LORD."
(Leviticus 23:23-25, AV)

This first festival of the second half is the feast of
trumpets. It typically indicates the arrival of royalty, of a
King. This usually would result in the gathering of
followers to be at one with their King, ten days later, as we
see below:

"26 And the LORD spake unto Moses,
saying,
27 Also on the tenth day of this seventh
month there shall be a day of Atonement:
it shall be an holy convocation unto you;
and ye shall afflict your souls, and offer an
offering made by fire unto the LORD.
28 And ye shall do no work in that same
day: for it is a day of Atonement, to make
an atonement for you before the LORD
your God.
29 For whatsoever soul it be that shall not
be afflicted in that same day, he shall be
cut off from among his people.
30 And whatsoever soul it be that doeth
any work in that same day, the same soul
will I destroy from among his people.

31 Ye shall do no manner of work: it shall
be a statute for ever throughout your
generations in all your dwellings.
32 It shall be unto you a sabbath of rest,
and ye shall afflict your souls: in the ninth
day of the month at even, from even unto
even, shall ye celebrate your Sabbath."
(Leviticus 23:26-32, AV)

This second festival is the feast of Atonement. It is
understood to have the connotation of at-one-ment.

Following this is the feast of Tabernacles:

"33 ¶ And the LORD spake unto Moses,
saying,
34 Speak unto the children of Israel,
saying, The fifteenth day of this seventh
month shall be the feast of tabernacles for
seven days unto the LORD.
35 On the first day shall be an holy
convocation: ye shall do no servile work
therein.
36 Seven days ye shall offer an offering
made by fire unto the LORD: on the eighth
day shall be an holy convocation unto you;
and ye shall offer an offering made by fire
unto the LORD: it is a solemn assembly;
and ye shall do no servile work therein."
(Leviticus 23:33-36, AV)

The third festival is then the Feast of Tabernacles.

The Fulfillment of the Holy Days and New Moon Sacrifices

There are many spiritual parallels in these festivals. We will concentrate on how Christ fulfilled the sacrifices of these festivals. We will provide a summary of these festivals here:

First half Spring festivals:

1) Passover
2) Feast of Unleavened bread, including the Wave Sheaf Offering
3) Pentecost

Second half Fall festivals:

1) Feast of Trumpets
2) Feast of Atonement
3) Feast of Tabernacles, including the Last Great Day

From Jewish insights, we need to understand something very important at this point.

The religious cycle starts with Passover in the first holy month and continues to the Feast of Tabernacles in the seventh month. However, the civil cycle starts with the Feast of Trumpets in the fall and continues through the spring festivals. There is a six month or half-year difference between the religious cycle and the civil cycle. The reader can verify this with any local Rabbi. This is very important to understand.

If we add the understanding of the religious cycle and civil cycle to the issue of the separation of Church and State, and Christ's role in all of this, we can begin to comprehend the interplay of events. For the sake of completeness, we will quickly deal with the issue of the separation of Church and State.

In the beginning of Israel's formation, religious issues were civil issues. Religious law was civil law. However, in the time before the Kings, Israel requested to have a human king just like the gentile nations, and God allowed this. Let's read how that came about.

> "4 ¶ Then all the elders of Israel gathered themselves together, and came to Samuel unto Ramah,
> 5 And said unto him, Behold, thou art old, and thy sons walk not in thy ways: now make us a king to judge us like all the nations.
> 6 But the thing displeased Samuel, when they said, Give us a king to judge us. And Samuel prayed unto the LORD.
> 7 And the LORD said unto Samuel, Hearken unto the voice of the people in all that they say unto thee: for they have not rejected thee, but they have rejected me, that I should not reign over them.
> 8 According to all the works which they have done since the day that I brought them up out of Egypt even unto this day, wherewith they have forsaken me, and served other gods, so do they also unto thee.
> 9 Now therefore hearken unto their voice: howbeit yet protest solemnly unto them, and shew them the manner of the King that shall reign over them.

10 And Samuel told all the words of the
LORD unto the people that asked of him a
king.”
(1 Samuel 8:4-10, AV)

This separation was allowed to happen and would
stay in effect, until Messiah would come to heal everything
and to reign over the earth. This question was posed to
Christ at his first advent about 2000 years ago.

“6 ¶ When they therefore were come
together, they asked of him, saying, Lord,
wilt thou at this time restore again the
kingdom to Israel?
7 And he said unto them, It is not for you
to know the times or the seasons, which
the Father hath put in his own power.
8 But ye shall receive power, after that the
Holy Ghost is come upon you: and ye shall
be witnesses unto me both in Jerusalem,
and in all Judaea, and in Samaria, and
unto the uttermost part of the earth.
9 And when he had spoken these things,
while they beheld, he was taken up; and a
cloud received him out of their sight.
10 And while they looked stedfastly toward
heaven as he went up, behold, two men
stood by them in white apparel;
11 Which also said, Ye men of Galilee, why
stand ye gazing up into heaven? this same
Jesus, which is taken up from you into

heaven, shall so come in like manner as ye
have seen him go into heaven."
(Acts 1:6-11, AV)

And so we see that Christ did not unite Church and
State at His first advent. He will, however, do this at His
second advent, when the saints will receive their reward, as
we see in Revelation:

"And they sang a new song, saying, You
are worthy to take the book and to open
its seals, for You were slain and have
redeemed us to God by Your blood out of
every kindred and tongue and people and
nation.
And You made us kings **and** priests to our
God, and we will reign over the earth."
(Revelation 5:9-10, MKJV)[Emphasis mine]

This has a bearing on the two different festival
cycles. The religious cycle starts in the first holy month, but
the civil cycle starts half a year later, in the seventh month.

Now we can add some incredible insight here.
When Christ first came, there should have been the
possibility to unite Church and State and to begin the
Kingdom of God in its fullness in Jerusalem. This was what
the Pharisees and other leaders feared. However, this would
not have been possible, given the general sinfulness of
humankind and the lack of faith. Hence there is the need for
the supreme Sacrifice to deal with human sinfulness first.
God cannot allow sinful and corrupt leaders in His
Kingdom.

So, Christ first came within the civil cycle of the Festivals, as the potential King of the Jews. However, He was rejected as King at that point by sinning mankind, and hence His exit from mankind started with the religious cycle to deal with sin at that point.

This truth concerning the birthday of Christ was hidden from humankind by the pagan festival of the returning sun, inviting the sun back to the northern hemisphere, on 25 December. This pagan festival was brought into the Church by some gentiles, and it was renamed and redone to become "Christian", and called Xmas. However, from the beginning of Christianity, this festival of Xmas was not practiced. Christ was not born on 25 December. In fact, the date of birth was obscured to prevent understanding in this respect. However, if we are going to understand how Christ fulfilled the sacrifices of the Holy Days, we will have to correct this misunderstanding. We will have to pinpoint the true date of birth of Christ, and it is nowhere near December! We will reveal the truth in the next chapter.

Unfortunately, to understand the sequence and then understand the spiritual sacrifices, we will have to do some detailed work in Chapter 2. Please take the time to work through it.

> "3 ¶ Through wisdom is an house builded;
> and by understanding it is established:"
> (Proverbs 24:3, AV)

We will do our best to prove the beginning point, from where Christ enters the picture and begins to fulfill the sacrifices. We will have to get all the facts together from various scriptures across your Bible.

"9 ¶ Whom shall he teach knowledge? and whom shall he make to understand doctrine? them that are weaned from the milk, and drawn from the breasts.
10 For precept must be upon precept, precept upon precept; line upon line, line upon line; here a little, and there a little:" (Isaiah 28:9-10, AV)

Once this groundwork is laid, the rest will flow easily, and the conclusion will come dramatically. From Chapter 3, it will flow more easily. Once read, the reader will marvel at the designs of our God. We can only stand in awe of our Savior, Jesus Christ.

Chapter 2

The date of birth of Jesus the Christ

The failure of Christianity to understand these events stems from a bit of paganism creeping into the true worship from the second century onwards. By the fourth century, the Roman Emperor Constantine claimed to have become a Christian and called together councils to decide on Christian practices. The practice of worshipping the sun in its return to the northern hemisphere called Saturnalia on the 25th of December was incorporated and Christianized to become Xmas. This was proposed as the date of the birth of Jesus.

However, this was according to the Roman calendar, which is now the general worldwide business calendar. God's calendar works differently. A glance at the Hebrew calendar will provide an idea of God's calendar. To begin to understand these things, we need to look at God's calendar, as we have seen in our quick study of Leviticus 23. Hence the average Christian would never have been able to understand how Christ fulfilled the Holy Day sacrifices. They have no idea of the Calendar of God as indicated in the Bible and practiced by the Hebrew people in their Jewish faith. Hence general Christianity is out of sync, and they are missing important markers.

The practice of Xmas is actually not new. It stems from old pagan practice. A visit to the local library resulting in a deeper study will reveal the truth. However, we can simply quote from your Bible. Notice how the prophet spoke against this pagan festival:

"1 ¶ Hear ye the word which the LORD
speaketh unto you, O house of Israel:
2 Thus saith the LORD, Learn not the way
of the heathen, and be not dismayed at
the signs of heaven; for the heathen are
dismayed at them.
3 For the customs of the people are vain:
for one cutteth a tree out of the forest, the
work of the hands of the workman, with
the axe.
4 They deck it with silver and with gold;
they fasten it with nails and with
hammers, that it move not.
5 They are upright as the palm tree, but
speak not: they must needs be borne,
because they cannot go. Be not afraid of
them; for they cannot do evil, neither also
is it in them to do good.
6 Forasmuch as there is none like unto
thee, O LORD; thou art great, and thy
name is great in might.
7 Who would not fear thee, O King of
nations? for to thee doth it appertain:
forasmuch as among all the wise men of
the nations, and in all their kingdoms,
there is none like unto thee.
8 But they are altogether brutish and
foolish: the stock is a doctrine of vanities."
(Jeremiah 10:1-8, AV)

Such is the origin of the practice of decking a tree with gold on the 25th of December. This is not the date of birth of Jesus.

To continue with this book, the reader has to come to terms with how Christianity lost first-century insights that the original apostles had. There are many proofs that Jesus was not born on the 25th of December. We will quickly provide some right here.

Remember that the 25th of December is in the middle of winter in the northern hemisphere. Shepherds will not allow their flock out in the freezing fields. They would rather have brought them into sheltered areas close to, and even into communal family buildings. But what do we find concerning the birth of Jesus?

> "8 ¶ And there were in the same country shepherds abiding in the field, keeping watch over their flock by night.
> 9 And, lo, the angel of the Lord came upon them, and the glory of the Lord shone round about them: and they were sore afraid.
> 10 And the angel said unto them, Fear not: for, behold, I bring you good tidings of great joy, which shall be to all people.
> 11 For unto you is born this day in the city of David a Saviour, which is Christ the Lord.
> 12 And this shall be a sign unto you; Ye shall find the babe wrapped in swaddling clothes, lying in a manger."
> (Luke 2:8-12, AV)

The shepherds were out in the fields at night. It can only be summertime, or at the latest late September or early October. A further indication is the timing of the decision of the Roman governor to have all the people counted and taxed in Israel.

> "1 ¶ And it came to pass in those days, that there went out a decree from Caesar Augustus, that all the world should be taxed.
> 2 (And this taxing was first made when Cyrenius was governor of Syria.)
> 3 And all went to be taxed, every one into his own city.
> 4 And Joseph also went up from Galilee, out of the city of Nazareth, into Judaea, unto the city of David, which is called Bethlehem; (because he was of the house and lineage of David:)
> 5 To be taxed with Mary his espoused wife, being great with child.
> 6 And so it was, that, while they were there, the days were accomplished that she should be delivered.
> 7 And she brought forth her firstborn son, and wrapped him in swaddling clothes, and laid him in a manger; because there was **no room for them in the inn**."
> (Luke 2:1-7, AV)[Emphasis mine]

Why would there have been no room for them in the inn? This was in Bethlehem, a day's journey from Jerusalem. What was the problem? We can understand this if we take into account that to reduce the disruption of the economy, it would have been wise to time this with the Jewish festivals since the people would be moving around towards Jerusalem anyway. The best time would have been at the end of the harvest, when the fall festivals were to occur. Notice the instructions according to the law:

> "16 Three times in a year shall all thy males appear before the LORD thy God in the place which he shall choose; in the feast of unleavened bread, and in the feast of weeks, and in the feast of tabernacles: and they shall not appear before the LORD empty:
> 17 Every man shall give as he is able, according to the blessing of the LORD thy God which he hath given thee."
> (Deuteronomy 16:16-17, AV)

It makes sense to have this all happen after the summer harvest, before the Feast of Tabernacles. Joseph and Mary would be on their way to Jerusalem anyway, and they would have found themselves at Bethlehem, near the Feast of Trumpets, which is the beginning of the fall festivals. The only problem is that there would be no space left at inns in Jerusalem, and the spillover would make their way to surrounding towns, particularly Bethlehem. So it is no wonder that when Josef and his family arrived in Bethlehem, there was no space left in any of the inns.

With the computer age came another discovery. The reader may be aware of the Bible Code. It was discovered that if the Hebrew characters of Bible books were sequenced and stacked into a two or three-dimensional form, then certain words would begin to form when one looks at how they line up in the matrix. From the Bible Code came the indication that Jesus was born on the first of Tishri. Many fascinating words emerge from a section of the Bible from Proverbs 15:16 to 17:16, when the Hebrew characters are stacked in a cube of 19 each. Some of the words that line up are Yosef, Miryam (Mary), Beit Lekhem (Bethlehem), Yeshua (Jesus), Son of man, born, Ruach (Holy Spirit), manher, shepherds, Angels and star. Among the words that line up in multiple directions are "on 1 Tishri". This is the first of the seventh month of the Holy Calendar, the Feast of Trumpets!

Some may not want to give the Bible Code much credibility, but it is still fascinating.

There is another definitive indication of the date of birth of Jesus. The great doctor Luke wrote down some history for us in the book of Luke, concerning the conception and birth of John the Baptist. From this, we can tie the scriptures together, and figure the birth of Jesus. Please notice the inscription concerning the priestly course of Abia, indicating when he would officiate. Let's see the incredible explanation in the Gospel of Luke:

> "5 ¶ There was in the days of Herod, the King of Judaea, a certain priest named Zacharias, of the course of Abia: and his wife was of the daughters of Aaron, and her name was Elisabeth.
> 6 And they were both righteous before God, walking in all the commandments and ordinances of the Lord blameless.

7 And they had no child, because that Elisabeth was barren, and they both were now well stricken in years.
8 And it came to pass, that while he executed the priest's office before God in the order of his course,
9 According to the custom of the priest's office, his lot was to burn incense when he went into the temple of the Lord.
10 And the whole multitude of the people were praying without at the time of incense.
11 And there appeared unto him an angel of the Lord standing on the right side of the altar of incense.
12 And when Zacharias saw him, he was troubled, and fear fell upon him.
13 But the angel said unto him, Fear not, Zacharias: for thy prayer is heard; and thy wife Elisabeth shall bear thee a son, and thou shalt call his name John.
14 And thou shalt have joy and gladness; and many shall rejoice at his birth.
15 For he shall be great in the sight of the Lord, and shall drink neither wine nor strong drink; and he shall be filled with the Holy Ghost, even from his mother's womb.
16 And many of the children of Israel shall he turn to the Lord their God.
17 And he shall go before him in the spirit and power of Elias, to turn the hearts of the fathers to the children, and the

disobedient to the wisdom of the just; to
make ready a people prepared for the
Lord.
18 And Zacharias said unto the angel,
Whereby shall I know this? for I am an old
man, and my wife well stricken in years.
19 And the angel answering said unto
him, I am Gabriel, that stand in the
presence of God; and am sent to speak
unto thee, and to shew thee these glad
tidings.
20 And, behold, thou shalt be dumb, and
not able to speak, until the day that these
things shall be performed, because thou
believest not my words, which shall be
fulfilled in their season.
21 And the people waited for Zacharias,
and marvelled that he tarried so long in
the temple.
22 And when he came out, he could not
speak unto them: and they perceived that
he had seen a vision in the temple: for he
beckoned unto them, and remained
speechless.
23 And it came to pass, that, as soon as
the days of his ministration were
accomplished, he departed to his own
house.
24 And after those days his wife Elisabeth
conceived, and hid herself five months,
saying,

25 Thus hath the Lord dealt with me in
the days wherein he looked on me, to take
away my reproach among men."
(Luke 1:5-25, AV)

After the end of the course of Abia, Elisabeth, the
mother of John the Baptist, conceived. When was this?
When was the priestly course of Abia, when the designated
priest did his duty? To find that out, we need to go back to
the Law of Moses, in your Bible. To get some guidance, we
will provide a quote from a Bible Commentary concerning
the verses in Luke:

"The large priestly tribe of Levi was
subdivided into twenty-four divisions, that
of Abijah (v5) being the eighth (1 Ch.
24:10). Each division did priestly duty at
the Temple for two weeks in the year, and
many of the priests spent the rest of the
year away from Jerusalem (v. 23) following
secular occupations."
(New Bible Commentary, Third Edition)

Abia was the New Testament name of the Hebrew
name Abijah. Let's look at the passage in 1 Chronicles 24:

"1 ¶ Now these are the divisions of the
sons of Aaron. The sons of Aaron; Nadab,
and Abihu, Eleazar, and Ithamar.
2 But Nadab and Abihu died before their
father, and had no children: therefore
Eleazar and Ithamar executed the priest's
office.

3 And David distributed them, both Zadok of the sons of Eleazar, and Ahimelech of the sons of Ithamar, according to their offices in their service.
4 And there were more chief men found of the sons of Eleazar than of the sons of Ithamar; and thus were they divided. Among the sons of Eleazar there were sixteen chief men of the house of their fathers, and eight among the sons of Ithamar according to the house of their fathers.
5 Thus were they divided by lot, one sort with another; for the governors of the sanctuary, and governors of the house of God, were of the sons of Eleazar, and of the sons of Ithamar.
6 And Shemaiah the son of Nethaneel the scribe, one of the Levites, wrote them before the King, and the princes, and Zadok the priest, and Ahimelech the son of Abiathar, and before the chief of the fathers of the priests and Levites: one principal household being taken for Eleazar, and one taken for Ithamar.
7 Now the first lot came forth to Jehoiarib, the second to Jedaiah,
8 The third to Harim, the fourth to Seorim,
9 The fifth to Malchijah, the sixth to Mijamin,
10 The seventh to Hakkoz, the eighth to Abijah,"
(1 Chronicles 24:1-10, AV)

So we know that during the eighth course of two-week services each, the dad of John the Baptist did service, and in the week after this, Elizabeth conceived. We have a starting point in time to work from here. If we count from the beginning of the Holy year according to God's calendar, the eighth course of two weeks was week 15 to 16.

To relate this to the modern calendar, we need to consider then that two courses are twice two weeks or 14 days, which is then 28 days. This almost relates to a month. The eighth course brings us towards the end of the fourth Holy month. The calendar of God starts in early April. This brings us to the month of August.

John the Baptist was conceived in August!

From this, we can look at another event. Let's continue in the book of Luke, from where we left off, in verse 26. Elizabeth conceived in August. She hid this reality for five months. This would bring us to January. In her sixth month, in February, she met Mary, the mother of Jesus. Notice what happened:

> "26 ¶ And in the sixth month the angel
> Gabriel was sent from God unto a city of
> Galilee, named Nazareth,
> 27 To a virgin espoused to a man whose
> name was Joseph, of the house of David;
> and the virgin's name was Mary.
> 28 And the angel came in unto her, and
> said, Hail, thou that art highly favoured,

the Lord is with thee: blessed art thou
among women.
29 And when she saw him, she was
troubled at his saying, and cast in her
mind what manner of salutation this
should be.
30 And the angel said unto her, Fear not,
Mary: for thou hast found favour with
God.
31 And, behold, thou shalt conceive in thy
womb, and bring forth a son, and shalt
call his name JESUS.
32 He shall be great, and shall be called
the Son of the Highest: and the Lord God
shall give unto him the throne of his
father David:
33 And he shall reign over the house of
Jacob for ever; and of his kingdom there
shall be no end.
34 Then said Mary unto the angel, How
shall this be, seeing I know not a man?
35 And the angel answered and said unto
her, The Holy Ghost shall come upon thee,
and the power of the Highest shall
overshadow thee: therefore also that holy
thing which shall be born of thee shall be
called the Son of God.
36 And, behold, thy cousin Elisabeth, she
hath also conceived a son in her old age:
and this is the sixth month with her, who
was called barren."
(Luke 1:25-36, AV)

The Fulfillment of the Holy Days and New Moon Sacrifices

These events all happened in February, the sixth month of Elizabeth's pregnancy. This month the Holy Spirit came to Mary, and she became pregnant with Jesus.

From conception to birth, normally takes eight months. If we count eight months from February, we come to the month of October. However, we need to remember that the Holy Calendar works by the lunar months, which is, on average, a day or two shorter than the modern calendar months. We need to discount about a day every month to gain more accuracy. If we do that over 14 months, we need to reduce the days by 14 days. Some would say we need to reduce it by as much as 20 days. Needless to say, this would then bring us to late September.

Several books have been written on this topic. The fact is that Jesus was born late September, perhaps even early October, depending on how the Holy Hebrew calendar matches with the modern calendar. This is very important to understand in the context of Jesus fulfilling the sacrifices of the Holy Days of Leviticus 23!

In October, we find a description of the fall sacrifices of Leviticus 23. The first Holy Day in the civil cycle is the Feast of Trumpets. If the possibility exists for Jesus to have been born on the day of Trumpets, it is highly significant! What does the Feast of Trumpets signify? What does the blowing of trumpets signify? The arrival of the King! The beginning of important events!

As we have seen earlier in this book, the holy days have two cycles according to Jewish understanding and practices. The civil cycle starts in the fall, with the Feast of Trumpets. The religious cycle starts in spring, with the Passover. Christ came as the King, being introduced into the civil cycle, as the anointed King, but was rejected. He then followed the religious cycle to deal with the sin of the people and was crucified on the Passover day.

You can see how it all works out. God does things according to a specific plan! He declared it thousands of years ago, and then it actually happened just as it was prophesied and written down by educated, literate prophets.

Chapter 3

The Sacrifice of the Feast of Trumpets

We now come closer to the understanding of the sacrifice of the Feast of Trumpets. This was the first sacrifice that Christ did. What was it?

We need to understand that Christ was a Son of God with God. He existed before the material creation. He had power over angels! He already had eternal life. In the universe, He had the highest position with God the Father! For Him to give it all up was a massive Sacrifice!

> "5 Let this mind be in you, which was also in Christ Jesus:
> 6 Who, being in the form of God, thought it not robbery to be equal with God:
> 7 But made himself of no reputation, and took upon him the form of a servant, and was made in the likeness of men:
> 8 And being found in fashion as a man, he humbled himself, and became obedient unto death, even the death of the cross."
> (Philippians 2:5-8, AV)

This was the first sacrifice of Christ, and it corresponds with the sacrifice of the Feast of Trumpets. The King was born, having sacrificed His eternal life, and power with God, so that He can be with humankind, to show us the way to eternal life! He had to become human, and subject to death, to prove the way to eternal life to us mortals.

> "9 But we see Jesus, who was made a little lower than the angels for the suffering of death, crowned with glory and honor, that He by the grace of God should taste death for every son."
> (Hebrews 2:9, MKJV)

And so Christ sacrificed His Glory with God the Father to become a human being. He gave up eternal life for a while, to be a human being in the flesh. This was a huge sacrifice.

> "1 ¶ And in the seventh month, on the first day of the month, ye shall have a holy convocation; ye shall do no servile work: it is a day of blowing the trumpets unto you.
> 2 And ye shall offer a burnt offering for a sweet savour unto the LORD; one young bullock, one ram, and seven lambs of the first year without blemish:
> 3 And their meat offering shall be of flour mingled with oil, three tenth deals for a bullock, and two tenth deals for a ram,
> 4 And one tenth deal for one lamb, throughout the seven lambs:
> 5 And one kid of the goats for a sin offering, to make an atonement for you:"
> (Numbers 29:1-5, AV)

This refers to the huge sacrifice that the Son of God made to become human. He arrived as our King. However He first had to deal with our sinfulness. He knew that humanity would kill Him to avoid the light of His perfect ways shining on our sinful lives. In this, we see our incredible sinfulness!

It was during this time of the Feast of Trumpets that another leader as a type of Messiah leads Israel into the Promised Land, by overcoming the fortress that was standing in the way. Joshua, a type of Jesus, finally breached the impossible, and with God's help, broke through the defenses, to begin the process of entering the Promised Land.

> "20 So the people shouted when the priests blew with the trumpets: and it came to pass, when the people heard the sound of the trumpet, and the people shouted with a great shout, that the wall fell down flat, so that the people went up into the city, every man straight before him, and they took the city."
> (Joshua 6:20, AV)

Also, during the restoration under Ezra and Nehemiah, we find that from the Feast of Trumpets, on the first day of the seventh Holy Hebrew month, the burned offerings began.

> "6 From the first day of the seventh month began they to offer burnt offerings unto

the LORD. But the foundation of the
temple of the LORD was not yet laid."
(Ezra 3:6, AV)

And so also on the Feast of Trumpets, the sacrifice of the
birth of the Messiah was shown in the sacrifice of the
priests in the Temple of God. Jesus Christ, the King,
sacrificed the glory that He already had, to become a
human being, to meet with us in person. What an incredible
entrance!

Chapter 4

The Sacrifice of Atonement

After Christ sacrificed His glory and security in His eternal existence with God, He could have enjoyed physical life as a human king in the flesh. He could have provided food security to all, and they would have loved Him for it. They could have lived a good life in the flesh, but that would have been temporary.

> "1 ¶ Then was Jesus led up of the Spirit into the wilderness to be tempted of the devil.
> 2 And when he had fasted forty days and forty nights, he was afterward an hungred.
> 3 And when the tempter came to him, he said, If thou be the Son of God, command that these stones be made bread.
> 4 But he answered and said, It is written, Man shall not live by bread alone, but by every word that proceedeth out of the mouth of God."
> (Matthew 4:1-4, AV)

Jesus could have enjoyed a very exciting and eventful life, knowing that He could have participated in all kinds of exhilarating and dangerous pursuits, yet without fear of early death.

"5 Then the devil taketh him up into the
holy city, and setteth him on a pinnacle of
the Temple,
6 And saith unto him, If thou be the Son
of God, cast thyself down: for it is written,
He shall give his angels charge concerning
thee: and in their hands they shall bear
thee up, lest at any time thou dash thy
foot against a stone.
7 Jesus said unto him, It is written again,
Thou shalt not tempt the Lord thy God."
(Matthew 4:5-7, AV)

He could have been among the gentile countries. He
did not have to be a Jew. If He was not circumcised, He
could have lived without having to obey all the Jewish
laws. He could have been a great ruler, expanding His rule
over other gentile countries. He could have become a world
ruler, two thousand years ago! He could have become
famous, and the world would have loved Him.

"8 Again, the devil taketh him up into an
exceeding high mountain, and sheweth
him all the kingdoms of the world, and the
glory of them;
9 And saith unto him, All these things will
I give thee, if thou wilt fall down and
worship me.
10 Then saith Jesus unto him, Get thee
hence, Satan: for it is written, Thou shalt

worship the Lord thy God, and him only
shalt thou serve."
(Matthew 4:8-10, AV)

Jesus could have had the world at His feet already
two thousand years ago. He could have replaced Caesar!
However, eternal salvation for humanity would not have
been possible—that required salvation by worshiping the
creator God.

God, the Father, had already made covenants with
the patriarchs that loved and obeyed Him. He had already
made promises to Abraham. He had already established the
covenant of circumcision with Israel. He had already
allowed Moses to establish the law of Moses, which
incorporated many prior laws, and the Commandments.
There had to be continuance. Jesus had to fulfill prophesies
inspired by the Holy Spirit. It all had to continue as
planned. God the Father has to be the Most High God, even
of Jesus Christ! Else the Word of God would have lost
some credibility!

Jesus had to be circumcised. He had to become a
Jew. He would then have been oppressed by the Romans.
Even the Jewish leaders would have opposed Him in order
to maintain their status. And He had to demonstrate perfect
obedience to all the laws of Moses all the time, besides the
Ten Commandments.

"17 ¶ Think not that I am come to destroy
the law, or the prophets: I am not come to
destroy, but to fulfil.
18 For verily I say unto you, Till heaven
and earth pass, one jot or one tittle shall

in no wise pass from the law, till all be
fulfilled.
19 Whosoever therefore shall break one of
these least commandments, and shall
teach men so, he shall be called the least
in the kingdom of heaven: but whosoever
shall do and teach them, the same shall
be called great in the kingdom of heaven.
20 For I say unto you, That except your
righteousness shall exceed the
righteousness of the scribes and
Pharisees, ye shall in no case enter into
the kingdom of heaven."
(Matthew 5:17-20, AV)

Jesus had to lead by example, to be able to say these
things. He had to endorse all that God the Father had
established before fully. From His birth, Jesus had two
possibilities before Him.

Consider the lavish lifestyle of a multi-billionaire
leader of a world empire. Compare that with the materially
depleted lifestyle of Jesus as an oppressed Jew in a Roman-
controlled state.

"19 And a certain scribe came, and said
unto him, Master, I will follow thee
whithersoever thou goest.
20 And Jesus saith unto him, The foxes
have holes, and the birds of the air have
nests; but the Son of man hath not where
to lay his head."
(Matthew 8:19-20, AV)

The decision to be a Jew stayed. Jesus never had any other desire but to be a Jew. He would fully obey the Heavenly Father's will. He would follow the predetermined procedures. He would fulfill all prophesies. Hence He sacrificed a lot of physical wealth, glory, and power that He could have gained, had He decided to give up being a Jew in an oppressed Roman world. This was His second great sacrifice.

Was the baby Jesus involved in the Feast of Atonement in His first few days on the earth? The Bible does not give us much indication in this regard.

However, in one of the early manuscripts that were not included in the Bible is a hint at a possible link. In a manuscript entitled "The First Gospel of the Infancy of Jesus Christ." we find something interesting.

> "Then after ten days they brought him to
> Jerusalem, and on the fortieth day from
> his birth they presented him in the temple
> before the Lord, making the proper
> offerings for him according to the
> requirements of the law of Moses: namely,
> that every male which opens the womb
> shall be called holy unto God."
> (Chap 2:5, I Infancy)

If the meaning of this passage is that ten days after His birth, they brought Him to Jerusalem, then there is a high probability that it was on the tenth day of the seventh holy month, the Feast of Atonement. And that would mean that Jesus as an infant, was there in the Temple as an at-one-ment sacrifice. He would have been circumcised two

days before, as per the law. Notice the covenant with
Abraham:

> "9 And God said unto Abraham, Thou
> shalt keep my covenant therefore, thou,
> and thy seed after thee in their
> generations.
> 10 This is my covenant, which ye shall
> keep, between me and you and thy seed
> after thee; Every man child among you
> shall be circumcised.
> 11 And ye shall circumcise the flesh of
> your foreskin; and it shall be a token of
> the covenant betwixt me and you.
> 12 And he that is eight days old shall be
> circumcised among you, every man child
> in your generations, he that is born in the
> house, or bought with money of any
> stranger, which is not of thy seed."
> (Genesis 17:9-12, AV)

So, it is quite possible that Jesus was circumcised
on the eight-day, and brought to the Temple before the
Lord as the at-one-ment sacrifice on the 10th day. Indeed
He would have been at one with His people, the
circumcised Israelites, children of Abraham, generally
called Jews at that time.

We can assume that in this Jesus did fulfill the
sacrifice, even on time. He was circumcised and would
perform His duties before God as a circumcised Jew,
keeping the festivals of God.

Chapter 5

The sacrifice of the Feast of Tabernacles

Shortly after the circumcision of Jesus, and their time in Jerusalem on the Day of Atonement, the Feast of Tabernacles would follow. We read of that in the book of Leviticus:

> "33 ¶ And the LORD spake unto Moses, saying,
> 34 Speak unto the children of Israel, saying, The fifteenth day of this seventh month shall be the feast of tabernacles for seven days unto the LORD."
> (Leviticus 23:33-34, AV)

Since Jesus and his natural parents were in Bethlehem at the time of the fall festivals, they would have stayed the 40 days till the purification of mother Mary would have been completed, according to the law.

> "2 Speak unto the children of Israel, saying, If a woman have conceived seed, and born a man child: then she shall be unclean seven days; according to the days

of the separation for her infirmity shall
she be unclean.
3 And in the eighth day the flesh of his
foreskin shall be circumcised.
4 And she shall then continue in the blood
of her purifying three and thirty days; she
shall touch no hallowed thing, nor come
into the sanctuary, until the days of her
purifying be fulfilled.
5 But if she bear a maid child, then she
shall be unclean two weeks, as in her
separation: and she shall continue in the
blood of her purifying threescore and six
days.
6 ¶ And when the days of her purifying are
fulfilled, for a son, or for a daughter, she
shall bring a lamb of the first year for a
burnt offering, and a young pigeon, or a
turtledove, for a sin offering, unto the door
of the tabernacle of the congregation, unto
the priest:
7 Who shall offer it before the LORD, and
make an atonement for her; and she shall
be cleansed from the issue of her blood.
This is the law for her that hath born a
male or a female.
8 And if she be not able to bring a lamb,
then she shall bring two turtles, or two
young pigeons; the one for the burnt
offering, and the other for a sin offering:
and the priest shall make an atonement
for her, and she shall be clean."
(Leviticus 12:2-8, AV)

And so the family of Jesus would have stayed near Jerusalem for 40 days from His birth so that the sacrifices for her purity could be fulfilled in the Temple.

> "21 ¶ And when eight days were accomplished for the circumcising of the child, his name was called JESUS, which was so named of the angel before he was conceived in the womb.
> 22 And when the days of her purification according to the law of Moses were accomplished, they brought him to Jerusalem, to present him to the Lord;
> 23 (As it is written in the law of the Lord, Every male that openeth the womb shall be called holy to the Lord;)
> 24 And to offer a sacrifice according to that which is said in the law of the Lord, A pair of turtledoves, or two young pigeons."
> (Luke 2:21-24, AV)

It stands to reason that since they would be in the vicinity of the Temple for 40 days, they would have been at the Feast of Tabernacles, which started on the 15th and continued till the 21st of that holy month. We can assume that the Jesus child would have been at least near the Temple at that time.

How would Christ have fulfilled a sacrifice during the Feats of Tabernacles? The scriptures are quite clear:

> "11 He came to His own, and His own received Him not.

> 12 But as many as received Him, He gave
> to them authority to become the children
> of God, to those who believe on His name,
> 13 who were born, not of bloods, nor of
> the will of the flesh, nor of the will of man,
> but were born of God.
> 14 And the Word became flesh,
> and **tabernacled** among us. And we
> beheld His glory, the glory as of the only
> begotten of the Father, full of grace and of
> truth."
> (John 1:11-14, MKJV)

Indeed Jesus came and "tabernacle" with us sinners. What does it mean? Let's understand this.

Christ sacrificed His glory and security with God to become flesh. Then He sacrificed the possibility of being a world ruler at that time to rather become a Jew in an oppressed Roman Israel. But as a Rabbi, He still could have lived a good life with honor as a teacher in the Temple. He naturally would have been respected, and would rather have mixed with the priests and their families. He was well respected as a teacher. Notice how Nicodemus approached Him.

> "1 ¶ There was a man of the Pharisees,
> named Nicodemus, a ruler of the Jews:
> 2 The same came to Jesus by night, and
> said unto him, Rabbi, we know that thou
> art a teacher come from God: for no man
> can do these miracles that thou doest,
> except God be with him."
> (John 3:1-2, AV)

Yes, Jesus could easily have stood up and isolate Himself to the priesthood, living among the priests, teaching in the Temple, and avoiding the sinners and downtrodden. But what did He do? He even sacrificed that to be among sinners, to be among ordinary folk. He even mixed with thieves and harlots! Even Jesus commented on this:

"31 And the Lord said, Whereunto then shall I liken the men of this generation? and to what are they like?
32 They are like unto children sitting in the marketplace, and calling one to another, and saying, We have piped unto you, and ye have not danced; we have mourned to you, and ye have not wept.
33 For John the Baptist came neither eating bread nor drinking wine; and ye say, He hath a devil.
34 The Son of man is come eating and drinking; and ye say, Behold a gluttonous man, and a winebibber, a friend of publicans and sinners!"
(Luke 7:31-34, AV)

To demonstrate this sacrifice, Jesus followed it up with a remarkable example, one that would change the nature of the ministry of God's servants:

"36 ¶ And one of the Pharisees desired him that he would eat with him. And he

went into the Pharisee's house, and sat
down to meat.
37 And, behold, a woman in the city,
which was a sinner, when she knew that
Jesus sat at meat in the Pharisee's house,
brought an alabaster box of ointment,
38 And stood at his feet behind him
weeping, and began to wash his feet with
tears, and did wipe them with the hairs of
her head, and kissed his feet, and
anointed them with the ointment.
39 Now when the Pharisee which had
bidden him saw it, he spake within
himself, saying, This man, if he were a
prophet, would have known who and what
manner of woman this is that toucheth
him: for she is a sinner."
(Luke 7:36-39, AV)

Jesus could have sided with the teachers of His day.
He could have isolated Himself from sinners like this
woman. But He sacrificed that privilege in order that
ordinary sinners may understand and experience the life of
the perfect Son of God, and in so doing, have His light
shine on them so that they can repent and change, and be
forgiven. He was the King that would rub shoulders with
sinners so that they would experience the perfect life of the
Son of God!

"40 And Jesus answering said unto him,
Simon, I have somewhat to say unto thee.
And he saith, Master, say on.

41 There was a certain creditor which had two debtors: the one owed five hundred pence, and the other fifty.
42 And when they had nothing to pay, he frankly forgave them both. Tell me therefore, which of them will love him most?
43 Simon answered and said, I suppose that he, to whom he forgave most. And he said unto him, Thou hast rightly judged.
44 And he turned to the woman, and said unto Simon, Seest thou this woman? I entered into thine house, thou gavest me no water for my feet: but she hath washed my feet with tears, and wiped them with the hairs of her head.
45 Thou gavest me no kiss: but this woman since the time I came in hath not ceased to kiss my feet.
46 My head with oil thou didst not anoint: but this woman hath anointed my feet with ointment.
47 Wherefore I say unto thee, Her sins, which are many, are forgiven; for she loved much: but to whom little is forgiven, the same loveth little.
48 And he said unto her, Thy sins are forgiven.
49 And they that sat at meat with him began to say within themselves, Who is this that forgiveth sins also?
50 And he said to the woman, Thy faith hath saved thee; go in peace."

"Luke 7:40-50, AV)

Jesus sacrificed His lofty position in Heaven to come down to us so that He could mix on an earthly plane with sinners. In this, He would save some from their sin! What a great King we have!

Chapter 6

Fulfillment of the Passover

Jesus Christ came in the first place as a king. He was promised to arrive and rule Israel in all justice and fairness. He of all beings would be qualified to do that. His fulfillment of the fall festival sacrifices already made Him special above all rulers that ever came, or may come. His disciples understood that from the scriptures. But it was not to be in His first advent.

After His death, it was clear that this goal may not materialize in the lifetime of those who followed Him then. Hence they finally asked Him directly:

> "6 ¶ When they therefore were come together, they asked of him, saying, Lord, wilt thou at this time restore again the kingdom to Israel?"
> (Acts 1:6, AV)

It must have been somewhat devastating to understand that it would not happen at that point. However, God had His reasons.

> "7 And he said unto them, It is not for you to know the times or the seasons, which the Father hath put in his own power.

8 But ye shall receive power, after that the
Holy Ghost is come upon you: and ye shall
be witnesses unto me both in Jerusalem,
and in all Judaea, and in Samaria, and
unto the uttermost part of the earth."
(Acts 1:7-8, AV)

Jesus was ready to rule, but the people were not
ready to follow and be ruled by Him. Not even His
disciples were ready at that point.   Jesus first had to deal
with sin! And some people had to overcome their personal
sin and receive power to stand up against the temptations of
the devil. They had to overcome fear, even the fear of self.
They had to overcome themselves. How would that be
possible?

Not even the apostle Peter had the power to stand
up for the truth and for his Leader and Teacher, not even
when knowing that He was the Son of God.

"13 ¶ When Jesus came into the coasts of
Caesarea Philippi, he asked his disciples,
saying, Whom do men say that I the Son
of man am?
14 And they said, Some say that thou art
John the Baptist: some, Elias; and others,
Jeremias, or one of the prophets.
15 He saith unto them, But whom say ye
that I am?
16 And Simon Peter answered and said,
Thou art the Christ, the Son of the living
God."
(Matthew 16:13-16, AV)

But even armed with this knowledge, Peter would still deny His teacher. Jesus knew this.

> "33 Peter answered and said unto him, Though all men shall be offended because of thee, yet will I never be offended.
> 34 Jesus said unto him, Verily I say unto thee, That this night, before the cock crow, thou shalt deny me thrice.
> 35 Peter said unto him, Though I should die with thee, yet will I not deny thee. Likewise also said all the disciples."
> (Matthew 26:33-35, AV)

But despite reassurances, this still happened.

> "69 ¶ Now Peter sat without in the palace: and a damsel came unto him, saying, Thou also wast with Jesus of Galilee.
> 70 But he denied before them all, saying, I know not what thou sayest.
> 71 And when he was gone out into the porch, another maid saw him, and said unto them that were there, This fellow was also with Jesus of Nazareth.
> 72 And again he denied with an oath, I do not know the man.
> 73 And after a while came unto him they that stood by, and said to Peter, Surely thou also art one of them; for thy speech bewrayeth thee.

74 Then began he to curse and to swear,
saying, I know not the man. And
immediately the cock crew.
75 And Peter remembered the word of
Jesus, which said unto him, Before the
cock crow, thou shalt deny me thrice. And
he went out, and wept bitterly.”
(Matthew 26:69-75, AV)

Something had to happen so that these future rulers
would overcome their fears and inhibitions. The real
problem was a lack of faith. They knew they were hopeless
sinners, and would not trust that they would overcome, and
be forgiven. They felt powerless. But they were called to a
higher duty:

“27 Then answered Peter and said unto
him, Behold, we have forsaken all, and
followed thee; what shall we have
therefore?
28 And Jesus said unto them, Verily I say
unto you, That ye which have followed me,
in the regeneration when the Son of man
shall sit in the throne of his glory, ye also
shall sit upon twelve thrones, judging the
twelve tribes of Israel.”
(Matthew 19:27-28, AV)

If they were to become rulers, they had to overcome
their fears. They had to overcome their sin, and know they
are forgiven. They had to have power over self and their

circumstances. They had to be able to stand up and be counted. Something drastic had to be done.

Before the crucifixion, they were rather powerless. They would not have been able to take the Gospel and expand the Kingdom of God beyond what Jesus achieved.

Two things had to happen, and they go hand in hand.

Firstly, they had to overcome their fears. To do that, they had to have favor with God. They had to be forgiven and be passed over. At this point, they were coming closer to being rulers in the eternal Kingdom of God. They were coming closer to receiving eternal life. But past sin was still weighing heavily on their mind and spirit. Se they had to be "passed over". Past sin had to be forgiven, wiped aside, and they needed to be shown to be given a second chance, now with renewed faith in God, and the possibility of eternal life waiting for them. They had to be renewed in faith!

Secondly, Jesus had to go where no man did before. He had to show His unwavering dedication, love, and willingness to die for them. He had to do it first. In this, they would be passed over, past sin forgiven, given power in the spirit to overcome self, and so succeed and attain eternity.

They had to be passed over.

You see, at this point, the apostles were still under the death penalty for past sins. Hence they could sense that they still did not have eternal life at hand for them. However, they have grown to the point where they would deeply and fully appreciate the sacrifice of the Passover. They would understand that Jesus loved them fully, and His love would cover their past sins. He would cover them before God, and God would forgive their sins for the sake of His Son, Jesus Christ.

And so the Passover was at hand.

Just as with the other festival days, and special sacrifices happening on them, they would be given this signal, by having their Passover suffer death exactly on their Passover day, indeed the very hour. Let's look at that.

Israel was initially held bondage to Egypt. They were simply powerless to free themselves. God would show them a lesson that would stand for all time. Egypt, under the Pharaohs, was a type for sin. And Israel, indeed all people, needs to be freed from sin that holds us bondage to a useless life.

So, the first step was to be passed over by experiencing the awfully traumatic experience of the Passover. In this, we need to see our state of hopelessness, our state of dying. Israel would experience this in the land of Egypt.

"1 ¶ And the LORD spake unto Moses and Aaron in the land of Egypt, saying,
2 This month shall be unto you the beginning of months: it shall be the first month of the year to you.
3 Speak ye unto all the congregation of Israel, saying, In the tenth day of this month they shall take to them every man a lamb, according to the house of their fathers, a lamb for an house:

4 And if the household be too little for the
lamb, let him and his neighbour next unto
his house take it according to the number
of the souls; every man according to his
eating shall make your count for the lamb.
5 Your lamb shall be without blemish, a
male of the first year: ye shall take it out
from the sheep, or from the goats:
6 And ye shall keep it up until the
fourteenth day of the same month: and
the whole assembly of the congregation of
Israel shall kill it in the evening."
(Exodus 12:1-6, AV)

The evening was meant to be towards the going down of
the sun.

"11 But it shall be, when evening cometh on, he
shall wash himself with water: and when the
sun is down, he shall come into the camp
again."
(Deuteronomy 23:11, AV)

The first evening is before sundown. The second
evening is when it is dark.

"5 In the fourteenth day of the first month,
between the evenings, is the LORD's
Passover,
6 and on the fifteenth day of the same
month is the Feast of Unleavened Bread to
the LORD. You must eat unleavened bread
seven days.

7 On the first day you shall have a holy convocation. You shall do no work of labor,"
(Leviticus 23:5-7, AV)

The high day is on the 15th, and the Passover was killed the evening before when the sun begins to be low on the horizon.

Historically the high priest would kill the Passover lamb before the Temple at the 9th hour Hebrew time, which is 3 PM current western time. This was, in fact, the very hour on which Jesus died on the crucifix.

"44 ¶ And it was about the sixth hour, and there was a darkness over all the earth until the ninth hour.
45 And the sun was darkened, and the veil of the temple was torn in the middle.
46 And crying with a loud voice, Jesus said, Father, into Your hands I commit My spirit. And when He had said this, He breathed out the spirit."
(Luke 23:44-46, MKJV)

This happened on the 14th day, the preparation day before the high day, the annual Sabbath, the 15th.

"50 ¶ And behold, a man named Joseph, a councillor, a good man and a just one,
51 this one was not assenting to their counsel and deed. He was from Arimathea, a city of the Jews; and he also himself waited for the kingdom of God.

52 This man went to Pilate and begged the
body of Jesus.
53 And he took it down and wrapped it in
linen. And he laid it in a tomb that had
been cut in the stone, in which no man
had before been laid.
54 And that day was the Preparation, and
the Sabbath drew on."
(Luke 23:50-54, AV)

So Jesus died on the Passover day, on the very hour,
between the evenings. He was our Passover.

"7 ¶ Therefore purge out the old leaven so
that you may be a new lump, as you are
unleavened. For also Christ our Passover
is sacrificed for us."
(1 Corinthians 5:7, MKJV)

Nothing can be clearer. Jesus fulfilled the Passover
sacrifice. We can only stand in awe and fall on our knees
before such a sacrifice! He would die for us to comprehend
our sinfulness, and to shock us to repentance.

Through this act, we would die to our sin, and give
up our selfish ways, and seek Him and His ways in all
humility!

"6 ¶ For when we were yet without
strength, in due time Christ died for the
ungodly.
7 For scarcely for a righteous man will one
die: yet peradventure for a good man some
would even dare to die.

8 But God commendeth his love toward us, in that, while we were yet sinners, Christ died for us.
9 Much more then, being now justified by his blood, we shall be saved from wrath through him.
10 For if, when we were enemies, we were reconciled to God by the death of his Son, much more, being reconciled, we shall be saved by his life."
(Romans 5:6-10, AV)

This is the nature of the Passover sacrifice of Jesus Christ. He helps us from resistance in the heart and hence still subject to eternal death, to life through faith in Him, by taking the first step, and show His unwavering love in His death. In this, he reached out first, across the divide, to grab the hands of those who cry over our sinfulness, and that seek release from our sinful nature, and find salvation and eternal life, holding on to His guiding hand.

Jesus Christ fulfilled the Passover sacrifice absolutely and completely.

Chapter 7

Fulfillment of the Wave Sheaf Offering

Having fulfilled all that was required of Him in His sacrificial life, Jesus was fully qualified to continue with further fulfillments.

Jesus promised to fulfill the sign of Jonah.

> "38 ¶ Then certain of the scribes and of the Pharisees answered, saying, Master, we would see a sign from thee.
> 39 But he answered and said unto them, An evil and adulterous generation seeketh after a sign; and there shall no sign be given to it, but the sign of the prophet Jonas:
> 40 For as Jonas was three days and three nights in the whale's belly; so shall the Son of man be three days and three nights in the heart of the earth."
> (Matthew 12:38-40, AV)

The explanation of how Jesus fulfilled this requirement is explained in the book on the "Creator's

Time Matrix", and "Expanding the Sign of Jonah". He died before the annual Sabbath, the First day of the Feast of Unleavened Bread, and was raised by the end of the weekly Sabbath within this Feast of Unleavened Bread. In that year, the annual Sabbath was on a Thursday, and the weekly Sabbath was on Saturday.

We see how Jesus was indeed in the belly of the earth for three days and three nights. On the day after that weekly Sabbath, another event happened that is very significant. We will see here how Jesus Christ fulfilled the Wave Sheaf Offering.

Just after the Passover evening, the Feast of Unleavened Bread commenced and continued for seven days. This obviously stretched over a weekly Sabbath. The day after that weekly Sabbath was the day of the Wave Sheaf Offering. Israel had to wave this Wave Sheaf Offering. We will see that Christians also need to wave an acceptable Wave Sheaf Offering! Let us begin this discovery by looking at the law to the Levites in Leviticus 23:

> "9 And the LORD spake unto Moses,
> saying,
> 10 Speak unto the children of Israel, and
> say unto them, When ye be come into the
> land which I give unto you, and shall reap
> the harvest thereof, then ye shall bring a
> sheaf of the firstfruits of your harvest unto
> the priest:
> 11 And he shall wave the sheaf before the
> LORD, **to be accepted for you**: on the

morrow after the sabbath the priest shall
wave it.
12 And ye shall offer that day when ye
wave the sheaf an he lamb without
blemish of the first year for a burnt
offering unto the LORD.”
(Leviticus 23:9-12, AV)[Emphasis mine]

Is there a parallel in what Jesus did? Yes, indeed!
Let's noticed what happened after the resurrection of Jesus.
We will pick up on events from the Gospel of John:

"1 ¶ The first day of the week Mary
Magdalene came early to the tomb,
darkness still being on it, and she saw the
stone taken away from the tomb.”
(John 20:1, MKJV)

This was the day after the weekly Sabbath, the day
of the Wave Sheaf Offering being presented in the Temple.

"2 Then she ran and came to Simon Peter,
and to the other disciple whom Jesus
loved, and said to them, They have taken
away the Lord out of the tomb, and we do
not know where they have laid Him.
3 Therefore Peter and that other disciple
went forth and came to the tomb.
4 So they both ran together. And the other
disciple outran Peter and came first to the
tomb.

5 And stooping down he saw the linens
lying, yet he did not go in.
6 Then Simon Peter came following him
and went into the tomb. And he saw the
linens lying there.
7 And the grave-cloth that was on His
head was not lying with the linens, but
was wrapped up in one place by itself.
8 Therefore, then, that other disciple also
went in, the one who came first to the
tomb. And he saw and believed.
9 For as yet they did not know the
Scripture that He must rise again from the
dead.
10 Then the disciples went away again to
themselves.”
(John 20:2-10, MKJV)

Jesus had risen the evening before, and when Mary
came to the tomb before dawn, Jesus had already walked
out of the tomb. Now notice a very significant event.

“11 ¶ But Mary stood outside of the tomb,
weeping. And as she wept, she stooped
down into the tomb.
12 And she saw two angels in white sitting
there, the one at the head and the other at
the feet, where the body of Jesus had lain.
13 And they said to her, Woman, why do
you weep? She said to them, Because they
have taken away my Lord, and I do not
know where they have laid Him.

14 And when she had said this, she
turned backward and saw Jesus standing,
but she did not know that it was Jesus.
15 Jesus said to her, Woman, why do you
weep? Whom do you seek? Supposing Him
to be the gardener, she said to Him, Sir, if
you have carried Him away from here, tell
me where you have laid Him and I will
take Him away.
16 Jesus said to her, Mary! She turned
herself and said to Him, Rabboni! (which
is to say, Master!)
17 Jesus said to her, Do not touch Me, for
I have not yet ascended to My Father. But
go to My brothers and say to them, I
ascend to My Father and Your Father, and
to My God and your God."
(John 20:11-17,MKJV)

Jesus would not let her touch him at this point. He
was preparing to ascend into the Third Heaven to appear
before the throne of God. At the very time when the priest
in the Temple would present the Wave Sheaf Offering to be
accepted by God, Jesus was going to be presented before
the Throne of God, as an acceptable sacrifice for all
Christians! Why was this important? We will deal with that
shortly. Let's read on:

"18 Mary Magdalene came and told the
disciples that she had seen the Lord and
that He had spoken these things to her.

19 ¶ Then the same day at evening, being
the first day of the sabbaths, when the
doors were shut where the disciples were
assembled for fear of the Jews, Jesus
came and stood in the midst, and said to
them, Peace to you!"
(John 20:18-19, MKJV)

Remember the reference to this day also being the
"first of the Sabbaths". We will build on that information
shortly.

"20 And when He had said this, He
showed them His hands and His side.
Then the disciples were glad when they
saw the Lord.
21 Then Jesus said to them again, Peace
to you. As My Father has sent Me, even so
I send you.
22 And when He had said this, He
breathed on them and said to them,
Receive the Holy Spirit.
23 Of whomever sins you remit, they are
remitted to them. Of whomever sins you
retain, they are retained.
24 But Thomas, one of the twelve, called
the Twin, was not with them when Jesus
came.
25 The other disciples therefore said to
him, We have seen the Lord. But he said
to them, Unless I shall see the print of the
nails in His hands, and put my finger into

the print of the nails, and thrust my hand
into His side, I will not believe.
26 ¶ And after eight days the disciples
were inside again, and Thomas was with
them. Jesus came, the doors being shut,
and stood in the midst and said, Peace to
you!
27 Then He said to Thomas, Reach your
finger here and behold My hands; and
reach your hand here and thrust it into
My side; and do not be unbelieving, but
believing.
28 And Thomas answered and said to
Him, My Lord and my God!"
(John 20:20-28, MKJV)

When Jesus saw Mary on the morning of the day of
the Wave Sheaf Offering, Jesus would not let her touch
Him. But now things have changed. He was presented as
our Wave Sheaf Offering as an acceptable sacrifice for all
Christians. He was glorified in the Third Heaven. His
power and glory were restored. He regained capabilities He
had before. He could appear and disappear as before. He
could walk through walls, yet enjoy a meal of fish with
people, and have them touch Him. And this was all possible
for He was accepted as our acceptable Wave Sheaf
Offering!

What does it mean? Let's elaborate!

God created humanity to be His sons and daughters to
expand His family.

> "27 And God created man in His image; in
> the image of God He created him. He
> created them male and female."
> (Genesis 1:27, MKJV)

However, humankind sinned, and the relationship broke down, apparently irreparable. However, God would not give up, and the Messiah would come to restore the breach. But consider this:

Who on earth can God trust to not turn against Him? Which human can God fully trust always to follow Him, never to sin? Nobody! Who can turn this situation around? God needed someone that can fulfill the role of the Mediator.

Job lamented about this problem between him and God. He was scared of God since he was aware of his sinfulness, and he could not trust himself in a direct relationship with God. Notice the lamentation of his desperate situation:

> "28 I am afraid of all my sorrows; I know
> that You will not hold me innocent.
> 29 I have been condemned; why then
> should I labor in vain?
> 30 If I wash myself with snow water, and
> make my hands ever so clean,
> 31 yet You will plunge me into the ditch
> and my own clothes shall despise me.
> 32 For He is not a man, as I am, that I
> should answer Him, that we should come
> together in judgment;

33 there is no mediator between us, who
might lay his hand on us both."
(Job 9:28-33, MKJV)

However, such a mediator was being groomed.

There are several requirements for this Mediator. Firstly, the person must never have sinned against God. Even as a human being in the flesh and subject to temptation, and even death, the person must prove total loyalty. There never was such a human being, never will be, for we are all born into the sin of humanity, and we all have failed. But Christ was already sinless, and stayed sinless, even in the flesh. So He is a loyal, trustworthy mediator from God's point of view, considering that the Son of God already had experience in dealing with Satan for perhaps millions of years. God made this clear to the disciples on several occasions:

"5 While he yet spoke, behold, a bright
cloud overshadowed them. And behold a
voice out of the cloud which said, This is
My beloved Son in whom I am well
pleased, hear Him."
(Matthew 17:5, MKJV)

Secondly, the Mediator must have proven that He would not be influenced by inadequate human beings. He must be able to live with us, even with sinners of the worst kind, and yet be completely incorruptible by our sin. The tendency of humanity is to be brought down by bad friends. The Mediator had to prove that even while having compassion on our situation, He must not be tainted by our sin, our inabilities, our lack of faith, our tendency to sin, and our way of trying to bring a good example down to our level. Even when we try to tempt Him to take the easy way out and so defy the Father's Will, He must still stay the course.

> "31 And he began to teach them, that the Son of man must suffer many things, and be rejected of the elders, and of the chief priests, and scribes, and be killed, and after three days rise again.
> 32 And he spake that saying openly. And Peter took him, and began to rebuke him. 33 But when he had turned about and looked on his disciples, he rebuked Peter, saying, Get thee behind me, Satan: for thou savourest not the things that be of God, but the things that be of men"
> (Mark 8:31-33, AV)

Thirdly the Mediator must have experienced life in the flesh and have succeeded and been able to take our hand in the spirit, and drag us up towards God. And having done that must then be justified in being the final judge to say that He succeeded, and He tried to drag us into the Kingdom of God, but we were not interested, we did not try, we would not put forth the effort from our side.

We, like children, will always backslide when it comes to the perfection that God desires. But when Jesus gives us a hand in the Spirit and tries to drag us up, we cannot sit down and refuse to put forth the effort from our side. In this Jesus must then be qualified to be our judge

since He was here, and in the Spirit He still reaches out to
us!

> "30 Truly, then, God overlooking the times
> of ignorance, now He strictly commands
> all men everywhere to repent,
> 31 because He has appointed a day in
> which He is going to judge the world in
> righteousness by a Man whom He
> appointed, having given proof to all by
> raising Him from the dead."
> (Acts 17:30-31, MKJV)

Such a Mediator would then be acceptable between
God and us. We as humankind needed to have brought such
a Mediator and have presented Him to God, just as the
Levite priest would wave an acceptable Wave Sheaf
Offering to be accepted by God.

> "10 Speak to the sons of Israel and say to
> them, When you have come into the land
> which I give to you, and shall reap the
> harvest of it, then you shall bring a sheaf
> of the firstfruits of your harvest to the
> priest.
> 11 And he shall wave the sheaf before the
> LORD to be received for you. On the next
> day after the sabbath the priest shall wave
> it."
> (Leviticus 23:10-12, MKJV)

Indeed, Jesus the Christ was that offering, being
accepted and received from humanity, as the acceptable

Mediator. And it happened on the exact day and hour that the physical Wave Sheaf Offering was waved in the Temple! Jesus fulfilled this offering perfectly!

Chapter 8

Fulfillment of the Wave Loaves Offerings

The final fulfillment of the spring festivals involves the day at the end of counting fifty days, called Pentecost. Let's pick up from the law to the Levites:

"15 ¶ And you shall count to you from the next day after the sabbath, from the day that you brought the sheaf of the wave offering; seven sabbaths shall be complete. 16 To the next day after the seventh sabbath you shall number fifty days. And you shall offer a new food offering to the LORD.
17 You shall bring out of your homes two wave loaves of two-tenth parts. They shall be of fine flour. They shall be baked with yeast, firstfruits to the LORD.
18 And you shall offer with the bread seven lambs without blemish of the first year, and one young bull, and two rams. They shall be for a burnt offering to the LORD, with their food offering, and their drink offerings, a fire offering of sweet savor to the LORD.

19 Then you shall sacrifice one he-goat for
a sin offering, and two lambs of the first
year for a sacrifice of peace offerings.
20 And the priest shall wave them with
the bread of the firstfruits, a wave offering
before the LORD, with the two lambs.
They shall be holy to the LORD for the
priest."
(Leviticus 23:15-20, MKJV)

It is significant that a sin offering is included. As we will see, this offering includes repentant disciples. Jesus had almost fulfilled His sacrifice. In this final step, it transfers to some imperfect human beings, hence the need for a sin sacrifice. But let's follow the events in the New Testament.

Jesus appeared to the disciples for forty days until He was taken up into Heaven. That was ten days short of the fifty days to the Wave Loaves Offering. Notice the sequence in the first chapter of Acts:

"1 ¶ Truly, O Theophilus, I made the first
report as to all things that Jesus began
both to do and teach
2 until the day He was taken up, having
given directions to the apostles whom He
chose, through the Holy Spirit;
3 to whom He also presented Himself
living after His suffering by many infallible
proofs, being seen by them through forty
days, and speaking of the things
pertaining to the kingdom of God."
(Acts 1:1-3, MKJV)

Jesus was only with them for forty days. He was not with them all the way for the fifty days. He left ten days short, ascending to the Throne of God. This was done to allow the disciples to begin to take responsibility. Christ was beginning to hand the management of the day to day operations of the disciples over to them. He would grant them the insight, motivation, and the power of the Holy Spirit, so that they could become apostles, and take over leadership to some extent.

"4 And having met with them, He commanded them not to depart from Jerusalem, but to await the promise of the Father which you heard from Me.
5 For John truly baptized with water, but you shall be baptized in the Holy Spirit not many days from now."
(Acts 1:4-5, MKJV)

This indeed happened ten days later. But first, the disciples had to experience the ascension.

"9 And saying these things, as they watched, He was taken up. And a cloud received Him out of their sight.
10 And while they were looking intently into the heaven, He having gone, even behold, two men in white clothing stood beside them,
11 who also said, Men of Galilee, why do you stand gazing up into the heaven? This same

Jesus who is taken up from you into Heaven, will come in the way you have seen Him going into Heaven."
(Acts 1:9-11, MKJV)

Ten days later they were together on the Feast of the two Wave Loaves, the feast of weeks, Pentecost.

"1 ¶ And in the fulfilling of the day of Pentecost, they were all with one accord in one place.
2 And suddenly a sound came out of the heaven as borne along by the rushing of a mighty wind, and it filled all the house where they were sitting.
3 And tongues as of fire appeared to them, being distributed; and it sat upon each of them.
4 And they were all filled of the Holy Spirit, and began to speak in other languages, as the Spirit gave them utterance."
(Acts 2:1-4, MKJV)

Now the disciples have become the apostles and were given boldness, motivation, and deeper insight and abilities to speak, even in other languages so that all could hear and understand. They were even given powers to do miracles, and to heal, just like Jesus!

After a powerful sermon by Peter, the results were astounding!

"41 Then those who gladly received his word were baptized. And the same day there were added about three thousand souls.
42 ¶ And they were continuing steadfastly in the apostles' doctrine, and in fellowship and in the breaking of the loaves, and in prayers.
43 And fear came on every soul. And many wonders and miracles took place through the apostles."
(Acts 2:41-43, MKJV)

Now the Gospel was spreading rapidly, and the Church grew by leaps and bounds! Three thousand members added in one day! And that after one sermon by Peter! Obviously, the sacrificing of Jesus Christ and the power of God through the Holy Spirit had much to do with the rapid growth. But the physical person that they now saw and stood in awe of was Peter.

Jesus Christ had the power to continue on earth. He was with them for forty days after His resurrection. He could have continued for years and years if He wanted to. But He gave some of the power over to the disciples, and they became apostles. They were raised to some extent to the level of Jesus, the man. And Christ gladly stepped aside and looked on with gladness and pride in the way these apostles continued. Christ happily sacrificed the status and position to receive daily worship and awe directly from human beings. He sacrificed that to hand over to the apostles to see the Church grow.

In the world, many leaders grow old and become fragile, even diseased. They should hand over, as health problems like Alzheimer's disease may set in. But many try desperately to hold on to that prestige and power to affect the day to day running of the governments they dictate to. But that was not the way of Jesus. He worked to have the deputies grow and succeed in the Work of God. He groomed them all along. He prepared them. And now, on the day of Pentecost, He did His final great act of sacrifice. He stepped out of the limelight. He disappeared from view. He handed over to the apostles and left them to continue, to receive some of the power that He had on the earth, and He did it gladly. What a great Leader!

Conclusion to Part 1

And so Jesus Christ fulfilled all His sacrificing on the earth. They all were quite contrary to the usual human ways of grabbing power and wealth for self. No, He came to fulfill the sacrifices of the law given to the Levites. And He had the power to sacrifice of Himself each time on the actual Holy Day of the sacrifice. He even had the power and humility to sacrifice Himself! He not only sacrificed Himself in the right way but on the exact dates, as predetermined by God thousands of years ago. Just how powerful, and how much control over events on the earth did God have to achieve this superhuman feat? No human being could have done that! Only God could have achieved this! How can any person doubt His existence! How can any person not believe?

Knowing that our Messiah did these great things on the Holy Days of the Hebrew calendar, we can expect this to continue.

When will Christ return?

Will He not continue with the sequence? Will He not return again on the Day of Trumpets, the same day that He was born from the Virgin Mary?

> "And immediately after the tribulation of those days, the sun shall be darkened and the moon shall not give her light, and the stars shall fall from the heaven, and the powers of the heavens shall be shaken. And then the sign of the Son of man shall appear in the heavens. And then all the tribes of the earth shall mourn, and they shall see the Son of man coming in the clouds of the heaven with power and great glory.
> And He shall send His angels with a great **sound of a trumpet**, and they shall gather His elect from the four winds, from one end of the heavens to the other." (Matthew 24:29-31, MKJV)

Is this the trumpet of the Holy Day of Trumpets?

> "¶ Behold, I speak a mystery to you; we shall not all fall asleep, but we shall all be changed;
> in a moment, in a glance of an eye, at the **last trumpet**. For a trumpet shall sound, and the dead shall be raised incorruptible, and we shall all be changed.

For this corruptible must put on
incorruption, and this mortal must put on
immortality."
(1 Corinthians 15:51-53, MKJV)

Some may say this refers to the trumpet of the seventh Angel in the book of Revelation, but the book of Revelation came after the writings of the apostle Paul to the Corinthians. So, unless Paul had foreknowledge of what was to be given to John, he could be referring to the time of the festival of Trumpets and hence indicating that Christ will return on the clouds on that very Holy Day.

This is some insight from the apostles of the first century. The Jewish Rabbis know about the last trumpet. We will do well to follow the Hebrew calendar. We may feel that Christ will return at the beginning of the fall festivals. We cannot be sure which year. Anyway, when we die, Christ returns for us that day, since at our next waking moment, we will see Christ. So we cannot play the game of seeking righteousness towards the feast of Trumpets, and if Christ did not return, we go back our own sinful ways for another year!

When Christ returns, He will return as the King of Kings, and the trumpet will announce the arrival of our Lord. He will not find Himself in a manger. This time He will come on the clouds.

"But in those days, after that tribulation,
the sun shall be darkened, and the moon
shall not give her light, and the stars of
Heaven shall fall, and the powers in the
heavens shall be shaken.

And then they will see the Son of man
coming in the clouds with great power and
glory.
And then He shall send His angels and
shall gather His elect from the four winds,
from the end of the earth to the end of
heaven."
(Mark 13:24-27, MKJV)

With love and dearness, knowing all His suffering
and sacrificing, we await His arrival at the last trump. What
a King! What a Mediator! The very Son of God!

Introduction to Part 2

We have seen how our Messiah sacrificed of
Himself, and finally Himself, on specific Holy Days, for us.
Even today, He is alive in Heaven and still sacrifices His
time and love to reach out to us in the Spirit, to save us
from our sin, and eternal death. How should we respond to
His sacrifices? What must Christians sacrifice in their lives
to come to Christ and receive eternal life? What is our role
in reaching out to eternal life?

Part 2 deals with our response and what we need to
do and become to reach out to God through the savings
Work of Jesus Christ, our Messiah.

The Law of Moses gives us further guidance into
the worship of God through Christ, our Heavenly Priest,
and His saving Work in the Heavenly Sanctuary.

We have to meet Messiah at His final sacrifice and
be moved towards repentance at the sight of what our sin
has done to Him. We have to die spiritually from our

former sinful self and begin our journey to salvation and eternal life.

> "Then Jesus said to His disciples, If anyone desires to come after Me, let him deny himself and take up his cross and follow Me.
> For whoever desires to save his life shall lose it, and whoever desires to lose his life for My sake shall find it."
> (Matthew 16:24 - 25, MKJV)

The Holy Days of Leviticus 23, Deuteronomy 16, and Numbers 28 to 29 give us further insight into our walk towards eternal life. Whereas Jesus sacrificed specific aspects of Himself and all His glory for our sake on the Holy Days, the Holy Days sequence also has guidance for us in reaching out to God through our High Priest. It has a dual purpose. There are sacrifices that Jesus did for us, and we must also feel moved to sacrifice our sinful self at various stages to be moved spiritually to Jesus Christ.

Section two deals with our response, and is pictured through the Holy Days and New Moons,

We can see that the earthly high priest had to repeat the sequence of sanctification on an annual basis due to continual sin, starting with the dedication of the temple at the first new moon of Nisan every year, from the Christian more perfection is required. We cannot be baptized over and over every year, rededicating ourselves, getting rid of the leaven of malice and deceit every year, after a lapse towards the end of the previous year.

"For Christ is not entered into the holy
places made with hands, *which are* the
figures of the true; but into Heaven itself,
now to appear in the presence of God for
us:
Nor yet that he should offer himself often,
as the high priest entereth into the holy
place every year with blood of others;
For then must he often have suffered since
the foundation of the world: but now once
in the end of the world hath he appeared
to put away sin by the sacrifice of himself.
And as it is appointed unto men once to
die, but after this the judgment:
So Christ was once offered to bear the sins
of many; and unto them that look for him
shall he appear the second time without
sin unto salvation."
(Hebrews 9:24-28, KJV)

So how do we allow Christ our High Priest to
sanctify us and purify us towards salvation on a permanent
basis? For us, as Christians, the journey is one way. We
cannot lapse to repent and redo our relationship on an
annual basis. We must repent and stay in a repentant
attitude, and build our relationship through successive
stages in a permanent way. We may slip and sin from time
to time, but we will immediately repent, seek forgiveness,
stand up, and continue the walk with Christ, overcoming
past sins. We cannot fall into a lapse, thinking that we can
be rededicated next year, baptized over again, and start
again. We cannot do this on an annual basis.

What is our walk with Christ, our perfect High Priest?

The annual sequence of the Law of Moses gives us guidance in our permanent walk with Christ towards the Kingdom of God, of which the first phase is the spiritual implementation in our lives now.

> "And when they had appointed him a day, there came many to him into *his* lodging; to whom he expounded and testified the kingdom of God, persuading them concerning Jesus, both out of the law of Moses, and *out of* the prophets, from morning till evening."
> (Acts 28:23, KJV)

Let's see what we can learn from the Law of Moses.

Chapter 9

Our dedication to the spiritual Temple

The first guiding light comes from the Apostle Paul, who told us that we are the Temple of God

> "16 Know ye not that ye are the temple of God, and *that* the Spirit of God dwelleth in you?"
> (1 Corinthians 3:16, KJV)

Therefore, the activities in the physical temple guide us to what should be happening in the mind, heart, and spirit of the believer.

The first new moon

First is the dedication of the temple. From the beginning days of the tabernacle in the desert, this was the case.

"And the LORD spake unto Moses, saying, 2 On the first day of the first month shalt thou set up the tabernacle of the tent of the congregation."
(Exodus 40:1-2, KJV)

When a new king was ordained over Israel, the temple was reopened, and the work of preparing for the worship of God started on the first new moon day.

"Now they began on the first *day* of the first month to sanctify, and on the eighth day of the month came they to the porch of the LORD: so they sanctified the house of the LORD in eight days; and in the sixteenth day of the first month they made an end."
(2 Chronicles 29:17, KJV)

So it is with us as Christians. Firstly we need to understand our calling. We need to understand the Gospel of the coming Kingdom of God, and we need to dedicate ourselves towards setting up our minds as the dwelling place of the Spirit of God.

"*There is* one body, and one Spirit, even as ye are called in one hope of your calling; One Lord, one faith, one baptism,"
(Ephesians 4:4-5, KJV)

We need to consider our lives and be prepared to rid ourselves of sin and prepare for obedience to the Commandments. We need to sanctify ourselves. This is the sequence.

"Elect according to the foreknowledge of God the Father, through sanctification of the Spirit, unto obedience and sprinkling

of the blood of Jesus Christ: Grace unto
you, and peace, be multiplied."
(1 Peter 1:2, KJV)

The Passover

"In the fourteenth *day* of the first month
at even *is* the LORD'S passover."
(Leviticus 23:5, KJV)

We find that Christ has fulfilled this law and has become
our Passover.

"Purge out therefore the old leaven, that ye
may be a new lump, as ye are unleavened.
For even Christ our passover is sacrificed
for us:"
(1 Corinthians 5:7, KJV)

Once a Christian is called by the message of the
Gospel, we prepare for the Covenant. That means the the
keeping of the Commandments. We set our hearts and mind
to please the Father in following Christ, and hence we are
ready to be passed over. We come to Calvary, to the event
that shows the result of our sin. Through the experience of
the crucifixion, we die to our sin, and so establish the new
Covenant. We need to come to Jesus.

"But ye are come unto mount Sion, and
unto the city of the living God, the
heavenly Jerusalem, and to an
innumerable company of angels,

> To the general assembly and church of the
> firstborn, which are written in heaven, and
> to God the Judge of all, and to the spirits
> of just men made perfect,
> And to Jesus the mediator of the new
> Covenant, and to the blood of sprinkling,
> that speaketh better things than *that
> of* Abel."
> (Hebrews 12"22-24, KJV)

So, we must die in spirit with Christ, and bury the old sinful self.

> "Buried with him in baptism, wherein also
> ye are risen with *him* through the faith of
> the operation of God, who hath raised him
> from the dead. "
> (Colossians 2:12, KJV)

We must be baptized in Christ, dying to the former self.

> "Know ye not, that so many of us as were
> baptized into Jesus Christ were baptized
> into his death? 4 Therefore we are buried
> with him by baptism into death: that like
> as Christ was raised up from the dead by
> the glory of the Father, even so we also
> should walk in newness of life."
> (Romans 6:3, KJV)

Baptism therefor, equates with being passed over, having died with Christ.

Feast of Unleavened Bread

"And on the fifteenth day of the same
month *is* the feast of unleavened bread unto the
LORD: seven days ye must eat unleavened
bread."
(Leviticus 23:6, KJV)

A further aspect of Christian growth is the need to become spiritually unleavened. Following the death of the former sinful self at baptism, we need to de-leaven ourselves. Christ often warned against the leaven of deceiving doctrines. One of the most serious forms of spiritual leaven is the deception of the self, trying to please God and follow Christ part-time. We can attend church, but may not have really repented, and may become guilty of malice in the Body of Christ eventually. We glorify in our knowledge but cause problems through superiority attitudes and other unchristian behavior.

"Your glorying *is* not good. Know ye not
that a little leaven leaveneth the whole
lump?
 Purge out therefore the old leaven, that ye
may be a new lump, as ye are unleavened.
For even Christ our passover is sacrificed
for us:
Therefore let us keep the feast, not with
old leaven, neither with the leaven of
malice and wickedness; but with the
unleavened *bread* of sincerity and truth."
(1 Corinthians 5:5-8, KJV)

Obviously, the Christian will not physically de-leaven one week every year as under the old Covenant, but will stay spiritually unleavened under the new Covenant. The whole event of baptism and laying on of hands must occur with the new convert being spiritually unleavened from deceit and the eventual malice that will occur if repentance was not true and sincere.

The Waive sheaf offering

"Speak unto the children of Israel, and say unto them, When ye be come into the land which I give unto you, and shall reap the harvest thereof, then ye shall bring a sheaf of the firstfruits of your harvest unto the priest: 11 And he shall wave the sheaf before the LORD, to be accepted for you: on the morrow after the sabbath the priest shall wave it."
(Leviticus 23:10-11, KJV)

Christ rose from the dead as promised. At the time of the Waivesheaf offering after Christ's crucifixion, certain spiritual events were to happen. Notice Christ's comments to Mary when He talked to her on this morning after the Sabbath.

"Jesus saith unto her, Woman, why weepest thou? whom seekest thou? She, supposing him to be the gardener, saith unto him, Sir, if thou have borne him

hence, tell me where thou hast laid him,
and I will take him away.
Jesus saith unto her, Mary. She turned
herself, and saith unto him, Rabboni;
which is to say, Master.
Jesus saith unto her, Touch me not; for I
am not yet ascended to my Father: but go
to my brethren, and say unto them, I
ascend unto my Father, and your Father;
and *to* my God, and your God."
(John 20:15-17, KJV)

Much happened this morning. Christ was raised, and the disciples went back and forth, as the news spread. The precise sequence is not under discussion here, but what is important was Jesus' statement. He mentioned that he must ascend to the Father. Revelation 5 gives us further insight as to what happened at the ascension. However, what is important to note is that the ascension happened at the same time when the Waivesheaf offering was waived by the earthly high priest in the temple that morning.

Christ was indeed waved as our acceptable Wavesheaf offering.

After baptism, we rise with Christ out of the watery grave, and so wave Christ as our offering, accepted on our behalf. We declare Christ as our role model, amongst other things when hands are laid on us. We accept Him as our first fruit.

"But now is Christ risen from the
dead, *and* become the firstfruits of them
that slept.

For since by man *came* death, by
man *came* also the resurrection of the
dead."
(1 Corinthians 15:20, KJV)

We, in effect, waive Christ as our perfect example of how we desire to be, and so declare that we seek Him to live in us, to bear fruit worthy of salvation. We demonstrate our faith in His salvation work for us in the Heavenly Sanctuary.

"Buried with him in baptism, wherein also
ye are risen with *him* through the faith of
the operation of God, who hath raised him
from the dead."
(Colossians 2:12, KJV)

Pentecost, the counting of the Omer

"And ye shall count unto you from the
morrow after the sabbath, from the day
that ye brought the sheaf of the wave
offering; seven sabbaths shall be complete:
Even unto the morrow after the seventh
sabbath shall ye number fifty days; and ye
shall offer a new meat offering unto the
LORD.
Ye shall bring out of your habitations two
wave loaves of two tenth deals: they shall
be of fine flour; they shall be baken with
leaven; *they are* the firstfruits unto the
LORD."

(Leviticus 23:15-17, KJV)

In the Talmud, a description is given of how to count the fifty days. It is known as the "counting of the Omer".

At baptism, hands are laid on us also in the name of the Holy Spirit. Counting the Omer refers to the new converts developing the Spirit in them from the first receipt at baptism.

> "Now he which stablisheth us with you in
> Christ, and hath anointed us, *is* God; 22
> Who hath also sealed us, and given the
> earnest of the Spirit in our hearts."
> (2 Corinthians 1:21-22, KJV)

From receipt of the Spirit, we need to stir up the Spirit.

> "Wherefore I put thee in remembrance that
> thou stir up the gift of God, which is in
> thee by the putting on of my hands."
> (2 Timothy 1:6, KJV)

This way, we fulfill the counting towards Pentecost, which symbolizes the fullness of the Holy Spirit in the formation of the Church of God.

Feast of Trumpets

> "And the LORD spake unto Moses, saying,
> Speak unto the children of Israel, saying,
> In the seventh month, in the first *day* of
> the month, shall ye have a sabbath, a

memorial of blowing of trumpets, an holy
convocation."
(Leviticus 23:23-24, KJV)

The blowing of trumpets demonstrates the crowning and
coming of the King.

> "And let Zadok the priest and Nathan the
> prophet anoint him there king over Israel:
> and blow ye with the trumpet, and say,
> God save king Solomon."
> (1 Kings 1:34, KJV)

So we also crown Jesus as our Lord and King in our
daily lives, when we submit to His way of love. We also
pray for His return to establish the Kingdom of God. We
also pool resources to preach the Gospel of the coming
Kingdom of God. So we blow the trumpet in our Christian
Work, declaring the coming of our King, and that Jesus is
Lord!

> "Wherefore God also hath highly exalted
> him, and given him a name which is above
> every name:
> That at the name of Jesus every knee
> should bow, of *things* in heaven,
> and *things* in earth, and *things* under the
> earth;
> And *that* every tongue should confess that
> Jesus Christ *is* Lord, to the glory of God
> the Father."
> (Philippians 2:9-11, KJV)

Atonement

> "Also on the tenth *day* of this seventh
> month *there shall be* a day of atonement:
> it shall be an holy convocation unto you;
> and ye shall afflict your souls, and offer an
> offering made by fire unto the LORD.
> And ye shall do no work in that same day:
> for it *is* a day of atonement, to make an
> atonement for you before the LORD your
> God."
> (Leviticus 23:27-28, KJV)

Christ has already made atonement for us.

> "For if, when we were enemies, we were
> reconciled to God by the death of his Son,
> much more, being reconciled, we shall be
> saved by his life.
> And not only *so*, but we also joy in God
> through our Lord Jesus Christ, by whom
> we have now received the atonement. "
> (Romans 5:10-11, KJV)

When He died at Calvary, the veil that was opened
on the day of atonement once a year by the earthly high
priest was torn in two, so we can be atoned through Christ,
our High Priest.

> "Jesus, when he had cried again with a
> loud voice, yielded up the ghost.
> And, behold, the veil of the temple was
> rent in twain from the top to the bottom;

and the earth did quake, and the rocks
rent;"
(Matthew 27:50, KJV)

So we as Christians who have the Holy Spirit and
have declared Christ as Lord and King in our lives can
attain access to the Father. Our prayers can indeed be
carried to the Most Holy God and Father of Jesus.

"And after the second veil, the tabernacle
which is called the Holiest of all;
Which had the golden censer, and the ark
of the covenant overlaid round about with
gold, wherein *was* the golden pot that had
manna, and Aaron's rod that budded, and
the tables of the covenant;
And over it the cherubims of glory
shadowing the mercyseat; of which we
cannot now speak particularly.
Now when these things were thus
ordained, the priests went always into the
first tabernacle, accomplishing the
service *of God*. 7 But into the
second *went* the high priest alone once
every year, not without blood, which he
offered for himself, and *for* the errors of
the people:
The Holy Ghost this signifying, that the
way into the holiest of all was not yet
made manifest, while as the first
tabernacle was yet standing:
Which *was* a figure for the time then
present, in which were offered both gifts

and sacrifices, that could not make him
that did the service perfect, as pertaining
to the conscience;
Which stood only in meats and drinks, and
divers washings, and carnal ordinances,
imposed *on them* until the time of
reformation.
But Christ being come an high priest of
good things to come, by a greater and
more perfect tabernacle, not made with
hands, that is to say, not of this building,
Neither by the blood of goats and calves,
but by his own blood he entered in once
into the holy place, having obtained
eternal redemption *for us.*"
(Hebrews 9:3-12, KJV)

So, we can come to God in boldness now, being
sure that our prayers will be carried to the holiest God by
Christ, who opened the way.

"Having therefore, brethren, boldness to
enter into the holiest by the blood of
Jesus,
By a new and living way, which he hath
consecrated for us, through the veil, that
is to say, his flesh
And *having* an high priest over the house
of God;
Let us draw near with a true heart in full
assurance of faith, having our hearts

sprinkled from an evil conscience, and our
bodies washed with pure water."
(Hebrews 10:19-22, KJV)

We can now be confident to have our prayers heard and
seek to become one with God.

Tabernacles

"And the LORD spake unto Moses, saying,
Speak unto the children of Israel, saying,
The fifteenth day of this seventh
month *shall be* the feast of
tabernacles *for* seven days unto the
LORD."
(Leviticus 23:33, KJV)

The apostle Paul indicated that we are the Temple
of God, and our bodies are then indeed considered a
tabernacle.

"Yea, I think it meet, as long as I am in
this tabernacle, to stir you up by
putting *you* in remembrance;
Knowing that shortly I must put
off *this* my tabernacle, even as our Lord
Jesus Christ hath shewed me."
(2 Peter 1:13-14, KJV)

If the Holy Spirit dwells in us, and we are the
Temple of God, then our bodies can become the Tabernacle
of God.

The next phase of fulfillment is when Jesus and His Father have found us acceptable as a person, and tabernacles with us.

> "Jesus answered and said unto him, If a
> man love me, he will keep my words: and
> my Father will love him, and we will come
> unto him, and make our abode with him."
> (John 14:23, KJV)

This way, we can fulfill the feast of tabernacles.

The Last Day

> "Seven days ye shall offer an offering made
> by fire unto the LORD: on the eighth day
> shall be an holy convocation unto you;
> and ye shall offer an offering made by fire
> unto the LORD: it *is* a solemn
> assembly; *and* ye shall do no servile
> work *therein*."
> (Leviticus 23:36, KJV)

After the feast of tabernacles, an eighth day was specified. This was the last day, on which Christ had the following to say:

> "In the last day, that great *day* of the
> feast, Jesus stood and cried, saying, If any
> man thirst, let him come unto me, and
> drink.

> He that believeth on me, as the scripture
> hath said, out of his belly shall flow rivers
> of living water.
> (But this spake he of the Spirit, which
> they that believe on him should receive: ...
> "

(John 7:37-39a, KJV)

When Jesus and His Father tabernacles with us, we will become true Christians, with the love of God flowing through the Holy Spirit in us out to others, in kind deeds and good works bearing the fruits of the Holy Spirit richly. Once we experience the love of the Holy Spirit in such a measure that we find ourselves manifesting the Love of God for others this way without having to be admonished or feeling forced to do good, we have indeed fulfilled the last day of the feast.

We can consider the meaning of each day of Leviticus 23, and ask ourselves how far we have come. At what point are we in spiritual development.

If we are true to our calling and stirring up the Holy Spirit in us, have we modified our lifestyles and homes so that we feel that Christ and His Father can tabernacle with us? If not, then we have not developed to the point of keeping the feast of tabernacles in spirit.

So, we can see how the festivals of the old Covenant can be seen as a barometer that will show us how far we have developed spiritually.

Every festival presents its own message, demonstrating a phase of development. This is a large subject, developed in the sermons of the Church.

We have seen how we can preach Christ out of the Law of Moses, in this case, Leviticus 23. Isn't it marvelous how every Word of God guides us towards perfection? There are messages in the ritual of the Law of Moses of the old Covenant of Israel, and it guides us into the Love of God. Blessed be Him who is doing everything for our sakes, to save us, and make us a part of His Kingdom!

Chapter 10

Fulfillment of the New Moons.

Introduction

From the Hebrew Calendar, we also see the New Moon festivals. In the book of Numbers, it was all spelled out in its procedures for Temple activities:

> "And in the beginning of your months you shall offer a burnt offering to Jehovah: two young bulls, and one ram, seven lambs of the first year without spot,"
> (Numbers 28:11, NKJV)

The beginning of the months had to be determined by observing the first faint crescent of the new moon just after sunset.

The practice was to have some people on the hills surrounding Jerusalem at the end of the 29th day of the month. They had to observe the horizon on the west once the sun went down. If the new moon was sighted, they would light a big bonfire, which would signal to those at the Temple that the new moon arrived, and celebrations would begin, and also sacrifices were made. Further away on other hilltops other observers would see the fires near Jerusalem and then light their bonfires. And so the signal would spread throughout Israel. This was a unified observance, and the calendar was maintained.

If the new moon was not sighted, the people that traveled to Jerusalem would stay over for the next night, at the end of the 30th day. Then the New Moon celebrations would happen. This way, there were at times two days reserved for the New Moons. Many Hebrew calendars still cater to this.

We can see this practice in the events between the younger David and the King of Israel that were not happy about the ascension of David to the throne. The King's son Jonathan liked David and helped him:

"And David said to Jonathan, Behold, tomorrow is the new moon, and I should not fail to sit at table with the King. But let me go so that I may hide myself in the field until the third day at evening."
(1 Samuel 20:5, MKJV)

Later we see in the events that there was a second day of the New Moon:

"And Jonathan rose from the table in fierce anger, and did not eat food on the second day of the new moon. For he was grieved for David, because his father had put him to shame."
(1 Samuel 20:34, MKJV)

Therefore the early Church – consisting of Jews and later gentiles – were keeping the Sabbath, Holy Days, and New Moons. The circumcised Jews certainly maintain the

Holy times as directed in the Old Testament Bible, attending Jewish synagogues when appropriate, and the gentiles had the privilege to also attend in the court of the gentiles in these synagogues wherever possible.

Paul indicated to them that they should not feel affected by others in their communities, judging them when they maintain the celebrations according to the Word of God.

> "Therefore let no one judge you in food or in drink, or in respect of a feast, or of the new moon, or of the sabbaths.
> For these are a shadow of things to come, but the body is of Christ.
> (Colossians 2:16-17, MKJV)

Therefore we see that the New Moons were also a shadow of things to come in the future and contained Godly wisdom. They had spiritual meaning on various levels.

We will now endeavor to delve into the spiritual fulfillment of the New Moons.

Be aware again that the time cycles of the Bible, as practiced by the Hebrew people of God, had two cycles. The religious cycle started with the month of Nisan, the month of the Passover, normally occurring in March or April of the pagan calendars. However, the civil cycle started from the seventh or in the eighth month of the religious cycle. This is after the month of the Feast of Tabernacles.

The religious and civil cycles can be considered to be about half a year apart. The reason for this is that Feast of Tabernacles is after the main harvest, in the seventh month. During this month of the Feast, the agricultural work is mostly done for the year, and farmers can now sell their produce after having given a tithe of the produce for the festival. The time has now started to sell products and buy implements for the next year. Now follows five months of business, selling, and buying. It was the start of civil business, after the seven months of agricultural and religious business.

A further issue was that the Feast of Trumpets on the New Moon of the seventh religious month indicates the arrival of the King. It is wonderful how the system works. Once the King has successfully cared for the food of his people, then he can have a celebration that heralds his arrival. The story is that only after he showed that he successfully cared for his people, can he be announced as the King with fanfare and trumpets. Then the civil cycle can begin with people concentrating on bartering and business according to the rules that the King established and maintained.

If the New Moons are to indicate the spiritual path of an individual to salvation, and the ultimate goal is to live forever in the eternal Kingdom of God, the end of that journey must be the Feast of Tabernacles, which is the culmination of spiritual and agricultural growth, being enjoyed in a time of plenty. Hence the start of the next cycle of meaning through the New Moon starts just at that point again. It starts in the civil cycle of five months and continues in the spiritual cycle of seven months. That is also how a person's life works out. We start as children in civil life and usually are much more concerned with physical things. However, later we become more religiously orientated and finally desire to enter the eternal Kingdom of God.

So the first New Moon of concern for the average person in the world that shows the beginning of our journey from civil life and becoming concerned about eternal life is the eighth New Moon. It is followed by the personal development walk of the first five months. This leads to repentance and forgiveness during the Passover or Crucifixion in the first religious month. Afterward follows the Christian growth for seven months towards perfection and entry into the joyous eternal Kingdom of God.

We will now look at that first New Moon of the eighth month, and uncover it's meaning for Christians.

Chapter 11

The Civil Cycle

Growing awareness

e will now compare the initial phase of a Christian's journey to eternal life, and how the first five New Moons have messages for the new Christian concerning the aspects that must be accomplished. These growth stages must be experienced and dealt with before adult baptism.

We know that baptism equates with experiencing the Passover and hence the Crucifixion of our Messiah. This happens in the first holy month, after the first New Moon. But before people go through with adult baptism, there are growth phases that must be done, as indicated by the eight to twelfth New Moon.

We will now start at the first New Moon of the civil cycle, the eight holy month of God's calendar.

The Eighth New Moon

The call to Godliness

It is no coincidence that God called the wayward people of Israel on the eighth New Moon to consider how far they are off the mark, having been corrupted by pagan practices in their commercial pursuits:

> **"In the eighth month**, in the second year of Darius, the Word of Jehovah came to Zechariah, the son of Berechiah, the son of Iddo the prophet, saying,
> Jehovah has been very angry with your fathers.
> And you say to them, So says Jehovah of Hosts: Turn to Me, says Jehovah of Hosts, and I will turn to you, says Jehovah of Hosts.
> Be not as your fathers, to whom the former prophets have proclaimed to them, saying, So says Jehovah of Hosts: Turn now from your evil ways and your evil doings. But they did not hear nor listen to Me, says Jehovah.
> Your fathers, where are they? And the prophets, do they live forever?
> But My Words and My statutes which I commanded My servants the prophets, did they not overtake your fathers? And they

returned and said, As Jehovah of Hosts
planned to do to us, according to our ways
and according to our doings, so He has
done with us."
(Zechariah 1:1-6, MKJV)[Emphasis mine]

The mission of the ministry of the prophet
Zachariah was given to him on this exact eighth New
Moon. The accusation from God is that the fathers of the
nation were engrossed in their commercial pursuits, and did
not listen nor considered the commandments of God. In the
following verses, God explained the red horse of war that
would come and destroy any gains they made because they
violated Godly principles.

For potential modern Christians, the call goes out to
turn to God. The pursuit of commercial interests can easily
lead to a wasted life. What will it gain any person if he or
she becomes rich only to die and lose out on eternal life?

God calls us out of our material life to consider our
ways and His better life of Godly principles, which will
lead to eternal life. God calls those in pagan religions to
study and prove who the real God is, and what the real
eternal religion is. Even modern Christianity has fallen into
the hands of commercial pursuits, and have been paganized
to the point of being ineffective, and unable to make one
wise unto salvation.

Out of all of these worthless and empty ways, God
calls people to consider our ungodly ways and to turn to the
true faith.

Most Christians may not be aware of how much
they have been compromised by paganism and commercial
interests. It takes a lot of studies to come to understand how
far the fathers may be off the mark. It could take many
months of full-time study to prove the true ways and true

religion. However, most people work hard and have limited time for Bible study. Few have time to spend in libraries. Hence this first phase of the walk to eternal life in the Kingdom of God could take several years for many working people.

The journey may be long. People must learn that the Sabbath is on Saturday, and Sunday churches are wrong in this regard. Xmas is from a pagan festival and not from Christ at all. Commercial Easter refers to the goddess of fertility, hence the Easter bunny and eggs. These symbols must be rooted out of any Godly worship. The Trinity doctrine was brought in by pagan teachers infiltrating the Christian faith. God the Father and Jesus Christ are two individuals in a fantastic relationship that leads to one purpose and goal. Shall we continue?

The Ten Commandments stand and need to be in our hearts and loved for all eternity. It is also the basis of the New Covenant. That includes the Sabbath command. Those who think all Biblical Law is done away lack understanding in dividing the Law of God. Shall we continue?

This is the meaning of the eighth New Moon, which is the first New Moon that future saints must fulfill.

Sadly many in the Churches of God have not even fulfilled this very important first phase. No wonder after many years in the Church, they are still swayed by the devil and sink back into paganized Christianity. They have never really fulfilled this New Moon.

The Ninth New Moon

Real worship

We are so busy with our financial and material pursuits. People ignored the need to do a serious investigation into their faith. Hence people pay no attention to God's Commandments and further guidance towards a holy life.

We think worshipping God means attending a gathering. We may think that singing a hymn may please God sufficiently so that we can go home and carry on the same old way. We even mistakenly called such gathering "worship services".

But true religion is far more than attendance on the Sabbath and singing. We need a change in thinking. We need to rectify our dealings with others. There are many things we need to learn. We need to change our ways through the week.

And so God wants us to realize this. Hence the message of the ninth New Moon is to bring this realization home to the people. Notice God's choice of timing when this realization comes through the prophet:

"And it happened in the fourth year of King Darius, the Word of Jehovah came to Zechariah in the fourth of **the ninth month**, in Chislev.
And Sherezer and Regem-melech and his men had been sent to the house of God, to seek the favor of Jehovah,

to speak to the priests who belong to the
house of Jehovah of Hosts, and to the
prophets, saying, Should I weep in the
fifth month, consecrating myself, as I have
done these many years? (Zechariah 7:1-
33, MKJV) [Emphasis mine]

The prophet indicated that even though an attempt
was made to please God through attendance and ritual, it
seems as though life has not improved. He fasted and
attended the ritual, but that did not help much. Problems
have not subsided. We are still beset with severe issues and
a threat to our very existence. And so God explains:

"And the Word of Jehovah came to
Zechariah, saying,
So speaks Jehovah of Hosts, saying,
Judge true judgment, and practice
kindness and pity, each man to his
brother.
And do not crush the widow or the
orphan, the alien or the poor. And do not
devise evil in your heart, of a man against
his brother.
But they refused to listen, and gave a
stubborn shoulder, and made heavy their
ears from hearing.
And they made their hearts adamant from
hearing the Law and the Words which
Jehovah of Hosts has sent through His
Spirit, by the former prophets. And great
wrath came from Jehovah of Hosts.

> And it will be, as He called, and they did
> not listen, so they called, and I did not
> listen, says Jehovah of Hosts. "
> (Zechariah 7:8-13, MKJV)

Attendance and ritual on the Sabbath are not enough. Fasting to humble ourselves is also not enough. We need to consider our ways through the week as well. All this needs to lead to more Christian life. And we need to learn that from God during Sabbath gatherings, and then take what we learned and do the Christian things through the week.

This realization of the depth of conversion and repentance is the message of the ninth New Moon, the second significant message on our road from an empty life to a Godly life that leads to eternal life in the Kingdom of God.

The Tenth New Moon

Unfortunate separation

Potential Christian saints have now understood that the true worship of God through Christ is given in detail in their Bibles. Other faiths are not acceptable. Paganized Christianity, full of pagan ideas and practices, is also not acceptable. God expects pure worship keeping His Commandments and finding mercy and forgiveness of past offenses through Christ.

Potential Christians also are now aware that the worship stretches into our ordinary lives through the week. How we treat other people and family is also at stake. The worship must lead to changed lives. It must lead to changes in attitudes and actions.

The message of the next New Moon brings us to the reality that, unfortunately, it may bring some separation from the world and its sinning population to some extent.

When the Temple was rebuilt in the days of Ezra, those that were to serve in its worship services had to be pure in life and associations. God will not allow any foreign influences or practices to have an effect. Unfortunately, some of the Levite tribe that would be designated as priests had married woman from pagan countries and cities. They were all now returning to Jerusalem under the grace allowed by God. But these pagan wives still brought pagan ideas and practices, and that could not be allowed in the Temple of God. Notice the timing of this awareness dawning on Ezra.
Ezra was seeking to find the answer to why God allowed some setbacks in the effort of building the Temple of God.

Notice when Ezra sat down with the other leaders to discuss the issue:

> "And let our rulers of all the congregation stand, and let all those who have taken strange women in our cities, come at a set time, and with them the elders of every city and its judges, until the fierce wrath of our God for this matter has turned from us.

Only Jonathan the son of Asahel and
Jahaziah the son of Tikvah made a stand
against this. And Meshullam and
Shabbethai the Levite supported them.
And the sons of the captivity did so. And
Ezra the priest, with certain heads of the
fathers, after the house of their fathers,
and all of them by names, were separated.
And they sat down in the **first day of the
tenth month** to examine the matter."
(Ezra 10:14-16, MKJV) [Emphasis mine]

Here is the crux of the meaning of the next New
Moon. It is the next message from God as we walk towards
eternal life. It is the realization that we may find some
separation from some people in the world.

Obviously, in the Christian era, no separation of any
marriages should happen. The Christian era is the spiritual
era. No physical separation should happen. But we may
find that the world for some reason may not like us
anymore. Notice the admonition from Jesus Christ:

"These things I command you, that you
love one another.
If the world hates you, you know that it
hated Me before it hated you.
If you were of the world, the world would
love its own. But because you are not of
the world, but I have chosen you out of
the world, therefore the world hates you."
(John 15:17-19, MKJV)

Unfortunately, the true worship and Christian life will separate us from former friends. We may find that former business associates become alarmed by our sudden newfound moral values. We will lose friendship with our drinking pals. We are no more getting stuck in a pub Friday night. During our new and pure life, some people may feel that our pious ways are not what they want to associate with. Unfortunately, there will be separation to some extent. It is inevitable.

Are we willing to separate from prior friends caught up in sin if there is no way out?

This is the decision we must make. Expect some separation as we begin to live the Christian life. We must be prepared for this, and deal with it mercifully, wisely and gently. Who knows when friends may appreciate our new life, and actually joins us in our walk to salvation?

> "But the servant of the Lord must not
> strive, but to be gentle to all, apt to teach,
> patient,
> in meekness instructing those who
> oppose, if perhaps God will give them
> repentance to the acknowledging of the
> truth,"
> (2 Titus 2:25, MKJV)

This is the great awareness and message of the tenth New Moon, the third message to those who discovered the true Faith.

The Eleventh New Moon

Expect difficulties.

If we can come out of other religions proving the true worship, and even uncover and come out of paganized Christianity, and we can deal with and accept the depth of changes required in our lives, and we can accept that possibly we may lose some friendships, the next message coming from the eleventh New Moon is to understand that our future road may be more difficult than what the average person experience in their normal lives. In fact, God is jealous of us and wants us to grow, often through calamities. Don't expect the road to salvation to be easy and plain sailing. We may experience a more difficult life than others.

The prophet Zechariah was called to preach to those that were forced to leave Jerusalem and Israel. Israel and Jerusalem experienced many wars. The poor Israelites experienced much more drama and even trauma than peoples from other nations. The Israelites did not understand how it is that they suffered so many calamities, while citizens of other pagan nations seem to have an easy life. Why was that? Was God not supposed to bless His people with peaceful existence? Notice God's answer, given in the eleventh month:

> "On the twenty-fourth day of
> the **eleventh month**, it is the month
> Shebat, in the second year of Darius, the
> Word of Jehovah came to Zechariah, the

son of Berechiah, the son of Iddo the
prophet, saying,
I watched by night. And behold! a Man
riding on a red horse, and He stood among
the myrtle trees in the ravine. And behind
Him were red, sorrel and white horses.
Then I said, O my lord, what are these?
And the angel who talked with me said to
me, I will show you what these are.
And the Man who stood among the myrtle
trees answered and said, These are those
whom Jehovah has sent to walk to and fro
through the earth.
And they answered the Angel of Jehovah
who stood among the myrtle trees, and
said, We have walked to and fro through
the earth, and behold, all the earth sits
still and is at peace."
(Zechariah 1:7-11, MKJV)[Emphasis mine]

So while the people of God suffer calamities, the
others have an easy time! Why was that? They have settled
and are at peace! Then comes the answer:

"Then the Angel of Jehovah answered and
said, O Jehovah of Hosts, how long will
You not have mercy on Jerusalem and on
the cities of Judah against which You have
cursed these seventy years?
And Jehovah answered the angel who
talked with me with good words,
comfortable words.

> So the angel who talked with me said to
> me, Cry out, saying, So says Jehovah of
> Hosts: I am jealous for Jerusalem and for
> Zion with a great jealousy.
> And with great anger I am angry at the
> nations at ease; in that I was but a little
> angry, and they gave help for evil.
> Therefore so says Jehovah: I have
> returned to Jerusalem with mercies. My
> house shall be built in it, says Jehovah of
> Hosts. And a line shall be stretched over
> Jerusalem."
> (Zechariah 1:12-16, MKJV)

Zechariah was promised that after the calamities that will bring the people to repentance, God would bring them to build a new physical Temple, and they will once day settle down and live a peaceful life in and around Jerusalem. For Christians, the promise is for the building of the Spiritual Temple, the Church of God.

God is jealous of His people. He does take notice of the plight of His people. While calamities help us to deepen our resolve to repent from sin and walk the Christian path, we need to build Faith that God is building His spiritual Temple, and one day the saints will be the building blocks in the government of the New Jerusalem. In the End Times, the peoples of the world will have their troubles, but the people of God will have joy as they look forward to the return of the Messiah and His promises, and eternal life in the Kingdom of God.

This is a big subject that needs extensive Bible study. However, the message of the eleventh New Moon is that we may have to trade the easy life in a sinning world with a more difficult life that may often be in conflict with the sinning world. But there is a promise and a hope of a coming fantastic life after the return of Messiah, and being settled in the future New Jerusalem.

The original Apostles had a very difficult time and was persecuted by their own people, more than we may experience in our life. They suffered the same kind of difficulties as the Israelites of old who were driven from Jerusalem and Israel. However, notice Jesus Christ's promises to them:

> "And Peter said, Lo, we have left all and
> have followed You.
> And He said to them, Truly I say to you,
> There is no one who has left house, or
> parents, or brothers, or wife, or children
> for the sake of the kingdom of God,
> who shall not receive many times more in
> this present time, and, in the world to
> come everlasting life."
> (Luke 18:28-30, MKJV)

Peter was promised that as an Apostle many people would offer rooms in their homes to him, and in the life to come to a permanent place in the glorious New Jerusalem

The message is this: can we have Faith, and endure calamities, learning and growing stronger in the process, and walk the road of Faith?

This is the message of the eleventh New Moon. Future Saints in Christ must ask themselves if they can accept this, for if they can, God holds out a fantastic future for them. But the road may be a bumpy one.

The Twelfth New Moon

Trust in God.

Having been converted, and understanding the depth of repentance, knowing that we may lose friends, and the road will not be easy, we need to receive some assurance that we are not alone.

We will begin a spiritual battle with the forces of darkness. We will find opposition to our new walk of Faith, and some may even set a trap for us to deter us.

But we can know that God is with us.

Before we take a step towards baptism, we are given assurances that if we stay the course, we will prevail. The story that applies to the new Christian is in the book of Esther.

Jews were removed from the Promised Land and were under threat of some of the leadership of their country of captivity. Through circumstances, the King got his eyes on Esther, which was from Judea. He wanted her in his palaces as one of his wives. However, one of the local rulers was very unhappy about it. He developed a plan to have prominent Jews killed. A trap was set. The King was trapped into making disastrous proclamations.

Notice the message from the twelfth month:

"And the letters were sent by postal riders
into all the king's provinces, to destroy, to
kill, and to cause to perish, all Jews, both
young and old, little children and women,
in one day, on the thirteenth of **the
twelfth month**, which is the month Adar,
and to take what they owned for a prize."
(Esther 3:13, MKJV)[Emphasis mine]

This disastrous trap was eventually circumvented
with a declaration that the Jews had every right to fight
back against this atrocity with fear of repercussions from
the King:

"In them the King granted the Jews in
every city to gather themselves, and to
stand for their life, to destroy, to kill and
to cause to perish, all the power of the
people and province who desired to attack
them, little ones and women, and to take
what they owned for a prize,
on one day in all the provinces of King
Ahasuerus, on the thirteenth of
the **twelfth month**, which is the month
Adar.
The copy of the writing for a command to
be given in every province was announced
to all people, even that the Jews should be
ready against that day to avenge
themselves on their enemies."
(Esther 8:11-13, MKJV)[Emphasis mine]

And so the trap backfired. The Jews were given favor and had a great moral and combat victory over those that set a trap for them, to destroy their efforts at a godly life even in a strange country.

> "And in the **twelfth month**, the month Adar, on the thirteenth day of the same, when the King's command and his order came to be done, in the day that the enemies of the Jews hoped to have power over them; though it was turned around, so that the Jews had rule over the ones who hated them.
> The Jews gathered themselves in their cities throughout all the provinces of King Ahasuerus, in order to lay hand on any who sought their harm. And no man could withstand them, for the fear of them fell on all people.
> And all the rulers of the provinces, and the lieutenants and the governors and officers of the King helped the Jews, because the fear of Mordecai fell on them.
> For Mordecai was great in the house of the King, and his fame went throughout all the provinces. For this man Mordecai was going on and growing greater."
> (Esther 9:1-4, MKJV)[Emphasis mine]

New Christians will do well to read the story of Esther and Mordecai, and their distress, and eventual good favor and victory over those that threatened their life. The enemies hated their righteousness and honorary dealings with the King. Their Godly ways won the day over their enemies.

Christians also need to understand that once they start on their journey to eternal life, their righteous ways may upset others, who may want to set traps for them. The thing to learn is to stay the course. God's ways work best. We will be granted victory and protection. We must gain assurance of this.

We will do well to read and understand the lessons of Esther and Mordecai on the twelfth New Moon. New Christians will do well to gain assurance that God's ways work, and Christ will make them strong and help them through the calamities that may come. This is the vital message in the last month or stage of development before the serious events of the first month, such as baptism showing repentance and receiving forgiveness of past sins and rebellion against God.

Chapter 12

The Religious Cycle

Introduction

Having begun in the civil cycle, a new convert began to learn and understand our need for salvation. There is no acceptance of death. We can live forever. But we need to get serious about religion.

The convert will have gone through the various phases, as depicted by the New Moon messages. Once the new Christian is thoroughly converted, convinced of the uniqueness of the Christian Faith, have come out of deception and paganized Christianity, and have gone through the phases of getting serious and willing to face difficulties and stay the course, it is time to get serious about fulfilling the religious cycle.

The First New Moon

Get up and go.

The new Christian is now prepared to get up and tackle the spiritual journey to salvation. Now the real deeds of a Christian start with confidence and surety.

We find the same theme for the New Moon of the first month in the Bible.

Ezra had been preparing for the return to Jerusalem, to establish the Temple services again, after the Jews were granted leave by the gentile emperor to do so. Notice when Ezra got up and went:

> "For on **the first of the first month** he began to go up from Babylon, and on the first of the fifth month he came to Jerusalem, according to the good hand of his God on him.
> For Ezra had prepared his heart to seek the Law of Jehovah, and to do it, and to teach statutes and judgments in Israel" (Ezra 7:9-10, MKJV)[Emphasis mine]

This is the message of the first New Moon. The Christian will now get up and go on the spiritual journey to salvation.

Israel, at times, neglected the Temple services. Some allowed paganism to enter the Temple, much like paganism entered some Christian churches. Notice when a new king got the priests to start getting rid of strange and pagan things out of the Temple rooms:

"And the priests went into the inner part
of the house of Jehovah to clean it. And
they brought out all the uncleanness that
they found in the temple of Jehovah into
the court of the house of Jehovah. And the
Levites took it out to the torrent Kidron.
And they began to sanctify on **the first of
the first month**. And on the eighth day of
the month they came to the porch of
Jehovah. And they made the house of
Jehovah pure in eight days, and in the
sixteenth day of the first month they made
an end."
(2 Chronicles 29:16-17, MKJV)[Emphasis
mine]

So also, the new Christian will now clean out the
pagan ideas and practices. The Christian will sanctify their
life for Christ (set apart for holy purposes). The first
purpose is to repent from sin, which, on its basis, means
keeping the Ten Commandments for starters.

The quest will be to work towards the Passover in
the middle of the first month, which equates with the
Christian baptism.

"Do you not know that as many of us as
were baptized into Jesus Christ were
baptized into His death?
Therefore we were buried with Him by
baptism into death, so that as Christ was
raised up from the dead by the glory of the
Father; even so we also should walk in
newness of life."

(Romans 6:3-4, MKJV)

Then after baptism follows the Feast of Unleavened Bread, which points to the Christian cleaning out their lives, just as the Israelites cleaned out the Temple.

So the message of the first New Moon is clear. Once we have proven what the right and true Faith is, and have withstood the falseness of the world, and the doubts that came our way, we are ready to get up and go. We consider our ways and begin the process of cleaning out sin. We are working towards baptism and take that first step. We are going to die with Christ and be raised a new person, cleaned from past sins, and cleaning out our worship and way of life.

The Second New Moon

Become part of the Family.

The new Christian has now been baptized, showing that he or she has left the old life of weak religious practices and sin. The Christian has covenanted to keep the Ten Commandments and grow spiritually in the grace and knowledge that Jesus Christ through the Spirit of God leads us to. So it is time to become part of the Family of believers and be counted as a member of the spiritual Temple of God.

The apostle Paul rightly describes us as building blocks of the spiritual Temple of God:

"For of God we are fellow-workers, a field
of God, and you are a building of God."
(1 Corinthians 3:9, MKJV)

We are being built as part of the Building of God.
As the Israelites got together and built the Temple of God
in Jerusalem, so today, Christians are being built into the
Church of God. We need to understand that we are being
framed into a useful and strong part of the Church of God.

Paul again repeated that fact:

"Do you not know that you are a temple of
God, and that the Spirit of God dwells in
you?"
(1 Corinthians 3:16, MKJV)

Now that we were baptized, we cannot sit back and
think we are saved. We must join the program, so to speak.
We need to learn, practice, and be hardened in our resolve
to follow Jesus Christ in the Spirit.

In the same way, the Israelites had to work to form
the building blocks to build the physical Temple of God in
Jerusalem. This happened in the second month of the Holy
Calendar. And they counted and recorded the workers and
builders in the second month:

"And in the second year of their coming to
the house of God at Jerusalem, **in the
second month**, Zerubbabel the son of
Shealtiel and Jeshua the son of Jozadak,
and the rest of their brothers the priests
and the Levites, and all they who had

come out of the captivity to Jerusalem,
began. And they chose the Levites, from
twenty years old and upward, to set
forward the work of the house of Jehovah.
And Jeshua stood up together with his
sons and his brothers, Kadmiel and his
sons, the sons of Judah, to set forward the
workmen in the house of God the sons of
Henadad, with their sons and their
brothers the Levites.
And when the builders laid the foundation
of the temple of Jehovah, they set the
priests in their robes with trumpets, and
the Levites the sons of Asaph with
cymbals, to praise Jehovah, according to
David king of Israel."
(Ezra 3:8-10, MKJV)[Emphasis mine]

This happened from the second month when they
began to build the second Temple of God during the
restoration under Ezra.

This also happened hundreds of years before when
Israel came from Egypt to the Promised Land. God told
them to do this on the New Moon day of the second month:

"And Jehovah spoke to Moses in the
wilderness of Sinai, in the tabernacle of
the congregation, on the **first day of the
second month**, in the second year after
they had come out of the land of Egypt,
saying,
Take the sum of all the congregation of the
sons of Israel, according to their families,

by their fathers' house, with the number
of names, every male by their heads,"
(Numbers 1:1-2, MKJV)[Emphasis mine]

And this they did, numbering those that made it
through the desert that would build and protect the Temple
in Jerusalem:

"And they gathered all the congregation
on **the first day of the second month**.
And they declared their pedigrees
according to their families, by their
fathers' house, according to the number of
the names, from twenty years old and
upward, by their heads."
(Numbers 1:18, MKJV)[Emphasis mine]

This is the message of the second New Moon. We
have a spiritual building to build. It will take study and
practice to build. We need to live the Christian life, learn its
principles, and be hardened by resisting temptations, and
maintaining the righteous life. When we are hardened, we
can be placed in our positions and fulfill our God-given
role.

The Third New Moon

Become a royal Priesthood.

Christians have now converted, overcome doubts,
repented, baptized and is now part of the Church of God.

They feel now at home in the Church and fellowship with the saints. One can now settle in the new life, and carry on with the services and Bible studies, and Church activities. However, there is much more to learn, to do, and to become.

Christians should strive for so much more than this. Christians have the potential to become leaders in this life but, in particular, the future life in the coming Kingdom of God, when Christ returns in power to begin His rule from Jerusalem.

This means studying beyond the moral law and spiritual insights, to also how God would want civil law to be. How would a Kings and Royal Priesthood develop a glorious civilization where fairness and justice lead to equality, yet development and endless peaceful growth? To achieve this means the training of a future Royal Priesthood.

Notice the message of God to the people of Israel in the third month of their journey to the Promised Land:

> "In the **third month** when the sons of
> Israel had gone forth out of the land of
> Egypt, **on this day** they came to the
> wilderness of Sinai.
> And they journeyed from Rephidim, and
> came to the desert of Sinai, and had
> pitched in the wilderness. And Israel
> camped there in front of the mount.
> And Moses went up to God, and Jehovah
> called to him out of the mountain, saying,
> You shall say to the house of Jacob, and
> tell the sons of Israel:

You have seen what I did to the Egyptians,
and I bore you on eagles' wings and
brought you to Myself.
And now if you will obey My voice indeed,
and keep My covenant, then you shall be a
peculiar treasure to Me above all the
nations; for all the earth is Mine.
And you shall be to Me a **kingdom of
priests** and a holy nation. These are the
words which you shall speak to the sons
of Israel."
(Exodus 19:1-6, MKJV)[Emphasis mine]

The initial hope of God was that the Israelites
would not only be a nation to Him, obeying His laws, but
would later even lead other nations to a greater existence.

Today that hope is on Christians! Notice the
message to Christians from the apostle Peter:

"But you are a chosen generation, a royal
priesthood, a holy nation, a people for
possession, so that you might speak of the
praises of Him who has called you out of
darkness into His marvelous light;
you who then were not a people, but now
the people of God, those not pitied then,
but now pitied.
Dearly beloved, I exhort you as temporary
residents and pilgrims to abstain from
fleshly lusts which war against the soul,"
(1 Peter 2:9-11, MKJV)[Emphasis mine]

The Fulfillment of the Holy Days and New Moon Sacrifices

Whereas we keep the New Covenant of Ten Commandments in our hearts and live the lofty life of morally upright Christians, we are to prepare for the new life of being priests in the resurrected life when Christ has returned to Jerusalem. We are then just temporary residents in our current cities with its civil code, but we long for and study to prepare to function in the future Kingdom and to be priests in that Kingdom, leading others to the morally upright life.

After Exodus 19 follows the time when the Commandments were given again in Exodus 20, and also the Law of Moses, explaining the civil code that must be implemented in the Promised Land.

The Festival of Pentecost was also to be kept in the third month.

From the Feast of Unleavened Bread, just after the Passover, the Israelites would count seven times seven days, and on the fiftieth days was this feast. The Priesthood of that time leads in soul searching and seeking moral perfection day after day, seven times seven days. But on the fiftieth day in this time in the Exodus, the complete Law was given. Israel had to prepare to receive this body of Law. They had to have prepared themselves emotionally and spiritually, to be in the right attitude to receive all these instructions.

This was also the day in which the risen Christ was taken up into Heaven to rule the Church that would spread across the world in Spirit. The apostles also received the Spirit that would lead them to perfection, and grant them insight and understanding to desire God's Law.

All of this happened in the third holy month.

The message of the third New Moon is to look forward to our calling to become Priests in the coming Kingdom of God, and to prepare by studying the civil code given to Israel. This civil code contains things like the seventh Sabbath year, the year of release of slaves, and other merciful events. It also contains the fiftieth year of jubilee, when lost family land returns to the original families. There are so many lessons to be learned from this. Although we as uncircumcised Christians in other countries are not under the Law of Moses, we must prepare to function in such a society when Christ returns.

The message of the third New Moon is then that there is so much more to learn. We are to become a Royal Priesthood for God, to be led by Jesus Christ, to build a wonderful new society after our resurrection!

The Fourth New Moon

The Church must evangelize.

Christians have now converted, overcame doubts, repented, became baptized and are now part of the Church of God. They feel now at home in the Church and fellowship with the saints. One can now settle in the new life and carry on attending Sabbath services and fellowshipping, building a right relationship with God through His Son and the Church. They will be aware that

they are now practicing the pure Faith in communities that
are lost spiritually, and maybe like Israel was when they
were taken away into captivity and forced to settle among
gentile nations practicing different religions. To them and
us, a message from God was delivered in the fourth month:

> "And it happened in the thirtieth year, in
> the **fourth month**, in the fifth of the
> month, as I was among the captives by the
> river Chebar, the heavens were opened,
> and I saw visions of God."
> (Ezekiel 1:1, MKJV)[Emphasis mine]

After Ezekiel described what he saw, the message came to
him:

> "And He said to me, Son of man, stand on
> your feet, and I will speak to you.
> And the Spirit entered into me when He
> spoke to me, and set me on my feet, so
> that I heard Him who spoke to me.
> And He said to me, Son of man, I am
> sending you to the sons of Israel, to the
> nations, the rebelling ones who have
> rebelled against Me; they and their fathers
> have sinned against Me, to this day.
> And the sons are stiff of face, and hard of
> heart. I am sending you to them; and you
> shall say to them, So says the Lord
> Jehovah."
> (Ezekiel 2:1-4, MKJV)

Ezekiel was called by God to deliver messages to the captives of Israel that were in a strange county. God wanted the Israelites to understand their state of being captive and unable to worship God properly. They were used as cheap labor and prevented from reaching their God-given potential. The state of captivity takes away many freedoms. Ezekiel was being prepared for his future role.

People in the world, in general, are also captives to strange religious practices. They are in this state due to their sin, and generally, they don't even know it. Hence God separates from them. The Spirit of God is removed from them, and they are prevented from their God-given potential.

The messages that were given to Ezekiel to state what he must do, and the problems he may experience, and the messages he must deliver to the captive Israelites, are very much the same as God's message to developing Christians at this level of spiritual growth in the Church of God. The message has to be delivered. Most will not want to hear the message, but some will. We should not be concerned with their response. The important thing is that a message must be delivered. We must evangelize.

> "And you shall speak My Words to them, whether they will hear or whether they will forbear, for they are rebellious."
> (Ezekiel 2:7, MKJV)

We should not be concerned with the response. They may resist. They may refuse the message.

> "But the house of Israel will not listen to you, for they will not listen to Me; for all

the house of Israel are strong of forehead
and hard of heart."
(Ezekiel 3:7, MKJV)

We are to evangelize anyway. The goal is not to
convert them. The goal is mainly to give them a warning. If
calamity then strikes, they cannot say they were not
warned. That is the main goal.

"Son of man, I have made you a watchman
to the house of Israel. Therefore hear the
Word of My mouth, and give them warning
from Me.
When I say to the wicked, You shall surely
die; and you do not give him warning, nor
speak to warn the wicked from his wicked
way, to save his life; the same wicked one
shall die in his iniquity; but I will require
his blood at your hand.
Yet if you warn the wicked, and he does
not turn from his wickedness nor from his
wicked way, he shall die in his iniquity;
but you have delivered your soul."
(Ezekiel 3:17-19, MKJV)

Ezekiel had to go and warn a rebellious Israel.
However, we must also inform a rebellious potential
Christian nation. We have to get the message out to them.
We cannot just sit in our comfort in Sabbath services, be it
in halls or home groups. The warning must go out.
But do we know the warning? And can we do it as
individuals? Will it be effective?

In the Christian era, the way of evangelizing is gentler. It is by the Spirit, and not by physical might. The people are not in immediate danger, as was the case with Israel taken away in captivity. We are dealing with spiritual warfare, a battle for the mind. People have been taken captive by evil forces, by deceptive means and confused leaders that are off the track themselves.

In Matthew 13, Jesus gave many parables showing how the seed is planted in the minds of people:

> "And He spoke many things to them in parables, saying, Behold, the sower went out to sow.
> And as he sowed, some seeds fell by the wayside, and the birds came and devoured them.
> Some fell on stony places, where they did not have much earth. And they sprang up immediately, because they had no deepness of earth.
> And the sun rising, they were scorched, and because they had no root, they withered away.
> And some fell among thorns. And the thorns sprung up and choked them.
> And some fell on the good ground and yielded fruit, indeed one a hundredfold, and one sixty, and one thirty."
> (Mathew 13:3-8, MKJV)

We will do well to read the whole of Mathew 13.

In His time, Jesus was doing the sowing of truth from God. In our time, evangelists are doing the work, and sow through various ways, using media and the Internet, and through books and gatherings if possible. And we work together on this matter.

In Matthew 25, Jesus gave the parable of apostles being given talents and how they should work to increase talents. Talents here imply things of value; in other words, money. He showed how they should at least support one another if they feel unable to evangelize on their own.

> "And he who had received the one talent came and said, Lord, I knew that you were a hard man, reaping where you did not sow, and gathering where you did not scatter.
> And I was afraid and went and hid your talent in the earth. Lo, you have yours. His lord answered and said to him, Evil and slothful servant! You knew that I reaped where I did not sow, and gathered where I did not scatter,
> then you should have put my money to the exchangers, and coming I would have received my own with interest."
> (Mathew 25:24-27, MKJV)

Members can also spread the Word without offending when people come and ask of them concerning their Faith. Christians at this level will certainly begin to shine in their communities, when they can be seen as people with integrity, keeping the Commandments, and refusing to be taken into temptations. Such Christians will also have joy in their heart, knowing that there is a purpose in their lives, as they are on a journey to eternal life. Then when others are attracted to them, and come and ask them of their Faith, they can provide wise answers, and then also evangelize.

> "But if you also suffer for righteousness'
> sake, you are blessed. And do not fear
> their fear, nor be troubled,
> but sanctify the Lord God in your hearts,
> and be ready always to give an answer to
> everyone who asks you a reason of the
> hope in you, with meekness and fear;
> having a good conscience, that while they
> speak against you as evildoers they may
> be shamed, those falsely accusing your
> good behavior in Christ."
> (1 Peter 3:14-16, MKJV)

And so Christians can also evangelize when the opportunity is there.

So the message of the fourth New Moon is that it is unacceptable to put the knowledge and wisdom that we have grown to understand under a bucket. We have to work together and do our bit to evangelize.

The Fifth New Moon

Seek and desire the Kingdom of God.

Christians in the Church of God have gone through a whole process of growth. They love the Church of God and fellowship with the saints. They are helping the leadership in evangelizing efforts and even have enough knowledge to answer for their Faith to anybody that wants to know more. God loves them and wants them to move on in their spiritual growth. He wants them to arrive at the spiritual and emotional state where they desire the future Kingdom of God. They learn even the civil code that will be implemented from Jerusalem. Even though they don't have to keep the civil code and laws, they read up and study those, understanding that one day Jesus Christ will return and implement those once He lives in Jerusalem.

This was the state and mind of the prophet that was given the mandate by a big world power to rebuild the Temple in Jerusalem. The Israelites were taken captive and exiled long before that, due to their lack of obedience, and growing sin.

After given the mandate to build the Temple again, Ezra started his journey on the first New Moon, and after a long journey and many incidents where he learned and grew in his relationship with God, and repented of more issues, he arrived in Jerusalem on the fifth New Moon, ready and able to do what he was called to achieve:

> "this Ezra went up from Babylon. And he was a ready scribe in the Law of Moses, which Jehovah, the God of Israel had given. And the king granted him all he asked, according to the hand of Jehovah his God on him.

And there went up some of the sons of
Israel, and of the priests, and the Levites,
and the singers, and the gatekeepers, and
the temple slaves, to Jerusalem in the
seventh year of Artaxerxes the king.
And he came to Jerusalem in the fifth
month, in the seventh year of the king.
For on the first of the first month he began
to go up from Babylon, and on the **first of
the fifth month** he came to Jerusalem,
according to the good hand of his God on
him.
For Ezra had prepared his heart to seek
the Law of Jehovah, and to do it, and to
teach statutes and judgments in Israel.
And this is the copy of the letter which
King Artaxerxes gave to Ezra the scribe, a
scribe of the words of the commandments
of Jehovah, and of His statutes to Israel."
(Ezra 7:6-11, MKJV)[Emphasis mine]

Ezra was a scribe that dutifully had copied all the
laws, statutes, and precepts that God gave to His model
nation to implement. He had written it out in detail, and
knew it all. He was ready and able and burned with the
desire to implement it all.

Whereas Christians in other countries in the world
are not required to keep the civil code of Israel but live
under the civil code of their particular country, they will
consider the civil code of their future country that they will
live in after their resurrection. After their conversion,
repentance, baptism, and growth in the Church of God,
even helping with evangelism, God wants them now to

grow in the knowledge of the future civil code of Israel.
Notice Jesus' advice to His followers:

"Therefore do not be anxious, saying,
What shall we eat? or, What shall we
drink? or, With what shall we be clothed?
For the nations seek after all these things.
For your heavenly Father knows that you
have need of all these things.
But seek first the kingdom of God and His
righteousness; and all these things shall
be added to you."
(Matthew 6:31-33, MKJV)

We should not be overly concerned with material
things. Even the basics will be available in countries where
Christians live. God will bless those countries with enough
food and clothing for the sake of Christians that live among
their population. But God wants us to keep the
Commandments, and read up on the coming Kingdom of
God.

The Kingdom of God has wonderful ways of
organizing a society. The Sabbath year will see sections of
land left alone every seventh year in alternate years to
recover. Slaves will go free as well. Every fiftieth-year
families can regain lost farms without having to buy them
back. No politically connected family will grow so
enormously rich that they end up owning cities! The poor
will always have a way out eventually. Farmers will leave
the corners of their fields for the poor to feed their families.
Even animals will be cared for. Indeed the civil code of the
Kingdom of God will provide equality and liberation. It
will prevent eventual wars as the poor standup to the filthy

rich families. Cities will be spared the destruction of civil wars.

Godly farming methods will prevent disease and ensure food supply. A correct diet will ensure a healthy lifestyle. Unclean animals will be avoided, and disease will not spread. It will be great in the future Kingdom of God. But those that will one day live there must first learn to implement and maintain it. Notice the promise from God:

> "They shall not hurt nor destroy in all My holy mountain; for the earth shall be full of the knowledge of Jehovah, as the waters cover the sea."
> (Isaiah 11:9, MKJV)

This is a further development of Christians that God desires before we can enter the eternal Kingdom of God. This is the message of the fifth New Moon.

The Sixth New Moon

Build the House of God.

We arrive at the last New Moon before the arrival of the King Jesus Christ. We will now look at the message given just before that glorious event of the return of the Messiah.

For the message to Christians, we look at the book from the prophet Haggai. The whole book is a message to Christians in the last phase of their lives before the death and resurrection later at the return of Messiah, Jesus Christ.

Just as exiled Israelites found themselves in gentile countries, so also Christians find themselves in various countries with different religions around them. However, Christianity managed to grow into gatherings with some financial power to build churches. Notice the message:

"In the second year of Darius the king, in **the sixth month, in the first day of the month**, the Word of Jehovah came by Haggai the prophet to Zerubbabel the son of Shealtiel, governor of Judah, and to Joshua the son of Jehozadak, the high Priest, saying,
So says Jehovah of Hosts, saying: This people says, The time has not come, the time that Jehovah's house should be built. Then came the Word of Jehovah by Haggai the prophet, saying,
Is it time for you yourselves to dwell in your finished houses, and shall this House lie waste?"
(Haggai 1:1-4, MKJV)[Emphasis mine]

The situation is that people of God have been blessed and are living in houses, and feel content. They have achieved reasonable comfort and feel enough has been done.

But they forgot that more is to be done. Christians can become weary and sit back, not doing the last step that God expects from them. Hence there are problems that set in, and the production from all the hard work seems to fade.

Christians may forget that God has blessed them so that they have the means to build the House of God. For

Christians, this means building the spiritual House of God, the Church of God. It means gathering in congregations and fellowshipping. But it can also mean building a church building, a place for Christian worship.

> "And now so says Jehovah of Hosts: Set your heart on your ways;
> you have sown much and bring in little; you eat, but you do not have enough; you drink, but you are not filled with drink; you dress, but no one is warm; and he who hires out himself hires himself for a bag full of holes.
> So says Jehovah of Hosts: Set your heart on your ways.
> Go up the mountain and bring wood, and build this House; and I will take pleasure in it, and I will be glorified, says Jehovah. You looked for much, and behold, little! And when you brought it home, then I blew on it. Why, says Jehovah of Hosts? Because of My House that is waste, and you, each man runs to his own house."
> (Haggai 1:5-9, MKJV)

For Christians, this means building the organizational structure for the Church to function, to help Christians to grow in the Grace and Knowledge of our Lord and Savior, Jesus Christ. It must also lead to evangelizing, and a gathering to fellowship, where new members as babes in Christ can be attracted to. It becomes a spiritually safe-haven where people can go to, to escape the wiles of

Satan and the evil world, to find spiritual and even emotional rest.

The good news is that the people will become moved to build the spiritual House of God. Leaders need to plan and take steps to achieve this, and the people will get together and help.

> "Then Haggai, Jehovah's messenger, spoke the message of Jehovah to the people, saying, I am with you, says Jehovah.
> And Jehovah stirred up the spirit of Zerubbabel the son of Shealtiel, governor of Judah, and the spirit of Joshua the son of Jehozadak, the high priest, and the spirit of all the remnant of the people. And they came and worked on the house of Jehovah of Hosts, their God,"
> (Haggai 1:13-14, MKJV)

This wonderfully ties in with the next chapter of Haggai, which also ties in with the seventh New Moon and the Feast of Tabernacles of the seventh month. This will be discussed shortly.

To the Christian gathering, the message is the same. Get together in the assembly and worship God and fellowship with the saints. We need to build the spiritual building, even as we congregate in a physical building.

> "Let us hold fast the profession of our faith without wavering (for He is faithful who promised),
> and let us consider one another to provoke to love and to good works,

not forsaking the assembling of ourselves together, as the manner of some is, but exhorting one another, and so much the more as you see the Day approaching." (Hebrew 10:23-25, MKJV)

We need to be actively building the congregation of God, all the time. It is our calling now. It is also what keeps us from drifting into only working on our personal lives, and not growing the Church of God.

The Seventh New Moon

The King arrives!

We arrive at the last New Moon in the holy sequence. Of all the new moons, this is the greatest New Moon and hence is also an annual Holy Day.

"And in the **seventh month, on the first of the month**, you shall have a holy convocation. You shall do no laboring work. It is a day of blowing the trumpets to you."
(Numbers 29:1, MKJV)[Emphasis mine]

The blowing of trumpets signals the arrival of the King.

"With trumpets and sound of a horn make a joyful noise before Jehovah, the King.

> Let the sea roar, and the fullness of it; the
> world, and those who live in it.
> Let the floods clap their hands; let the
> hills be joyful together
> before Jehovah; for He comes to judge the
> earth; with righteousness He shall judge
> the world, and the peoples in
> uprightness.”
> (Psalm 98:6-9, MKJV)

It was even blown before the King of Israel. It was
also blown when the foundation of the Temple of God was
laid:

> “And when the builders laid the
> foundation of the temple of Jehovah, they
> set the priests in their robes
> with **trumpets**, and the Levites the sons of
> Asaph with cymbals, to praise Jehovah,
> according to David king of Israel.”
> (Ezra 3:10, MKJV)[Emphasis mine]

And who is the cornerstone of the Spiritual Temple of
God?

> “and are built upon the foundation of the
> apostles and prophets, Jesus Christ
> Himself being the chief cornerstone,”
> (Ephesians 2:20, MKJV)

And so the message of the seventh New Moon is
first that the Messiah will arrive, and that the spiritual

Temple will then come together on the Corner Stone, Jesus Christ. Then the Church of God will become the main Church in the entire world, and eventually the only Church. What was started by cell groups and later congregations will flourish and mushroom into glorious communities living in peace and harmony.

But in the current life, Christians gather to celebrate the future arrival of Messiah. We humble ourselves in fasting on the tenth of the month before the King, and we also celebrate at the Feast of Tabernacle.

New people who observe this celebration learns about the future arrival of Messiah, becomes interested in His coming Kingdom, and start the New Moon and Holy Days sequence as established Christians did before.

Lest look at Haggai 2, and see how the wonderful synchronized sequences complete.

> "In the **seventh month, in the twenty-first of the month,** the Word of Jehovah came by the prophet Haggai, saying, Now speak to Zerubbabel the son of Shealtiel, governor of Judah, and to Joshua the son of Jehozadak, the high priest, and to the remnant of the people, saying, Who is left among you who saw this house in her first glory? And how do you see it now? When compared to it, is it not as nothing in your eyes?"
> (Haggai2:1-3, MKJV)[Emphasis mine]

The twenty-first of the seventh month is the last day of the Feast of Tabernacles. The message is that the Church

that we build may not be as big and glorious as we may
have hoped for. We may have hoped more people will
come and assist and join in the benefits and experience. But
God wants to encourage us:

> "Yet now be strong, O Zerubbabel, says
> Jehovah. And be strong, O Joshua, son of
> Jehozadak, the high priest; and be strong
> all people of the land, says Jehovah, and
> work; for I am with you, says Jehovah of
> Hosts
> with the Word who cut a covenant with
> you when you came out of Egypt, and My
> Spirit remains among you. Do not fear.
> For so says Jehovah of Hosts: Yet once, it
> is a little while, and I will shake the
> heavens, and the earth, and the sea, and
> the dry land.
> And I will shake all the nations; and the
> desire of all nations shall come; and I will
> fill this house with glory, says Jehovah of
> Hosts.
> The silver is Mine, and the gold is Mine,
> says Jehovah of Hosts.
> The glory of this latter house shall be
> greater than that of the former, says
> Jehovah of Hosts. And in this place I will
> give peace, says Jehovah of Hosts.
> (Haggai 2:4-9, MKJV)

In the millennial rule of Christ, all people will
eventually join the Church of God and build it into a
worldwide universal organization. It will have billions of

members, much bigger and much more glorious than it is today.

Locally the whole neighborhood will join and attend the local Church. They will assist in building a huge building, and everyone will join in. What the few members have started will grow in the new millennium beyond our wildest dreams. God will do it.

The spiritual building that the mature members put together will lead to the return of Christ, and together the spiritual building will rapidly expand. But that is the story started by the seventh New Moon, and also completed by it.

"And behold, I am coming quickly, and My reward is with Me, to give to each according as his work is.
I am the Alpha and the Omega, the Beginning and the Ending, the First and the Last.
Bessed are they who do His commandments, that their authority will be over the Tree of Life, and they may enter in by the gates into the city."
(Revelation 22:12-14, MKJV)

What a great God we serve! What a glorious Messiah we follow! What wisdom and insight were given to us! What a sure path to salvation we can follow! We can be sure of our salvation and eternal life in the coming Kingdom of God.

As we go through these sequences, we learn and are built up as the spiritual Temple of God, just as the prophets did thousands of years ago. God established this for us. All we need to do is follow the process, and enjoy the exciting knowledge and wisdom, and live it year after year!

May His Kingdom come! Now and forever!

www.ingramcontent.com/pod-product-compliance
Lightning Source LLC
Chambersburg PA
CBHW030241160726

47987CB00020B/490